Mastering Eli Concurrency

Powering High-Performance Backend Applications

Edison Owen

Table of Contents

Preface

Hey there, fellow programmer! Excited about building powerful backend systems? Buckle up, because we're about to dive headfirst into the fantastic world of Elixir concurrency! This book is your roadmap to mastering this essential skill and unlocking the true potential of your applications.

Background and Motivation

We all know the frustration of sluggish backend systems. Users tapping their feet, servers groaning under pressure – it's not a pretty picture. But what if there was a way to build applications that are fast, responsive, and can handle anything you throw at them? Enter Elixir concurrency!

This unique approach lets you build applications that can handle multiple tasks simultaneously, making them incredibly efficient and scalable. It's like having a team of super-powered workers handling requests at lightning speed, keeping your users happy and your system humming along smoothly.

Purpose and Scope

This book is your comprehensive guide to mastering Elixir concurrency. We'll start with the basics, breaking down the building blocks like processes, messages, and supervision. Then, we'll delve into powerful patterns and techniques used by Elixir pros to create rock-solid backend systems. We'll cover everything from handling API requests concurrently to building fault-tolerant applications that can bounce back from any hiccup.

But this book isn't just about theory. We'll also explore real-world examples, showing you how to put these powerful concepts into practice. You'll learn how to tackle common backend tasks – like interacting with databases and processing background jobs – with the power of concurrency at your fingertips.

Target Audience

This book is perfect for programmers who are familiar with the basics of Elixir and want to take their skills to the next level. Whether you're building a simple web application or a complex backend system, mastering concurrency will give you the tools you need to create truly exceptional software.

Organization and Structure

We've structured the book in a clear and logical way, starting with the fundamentals and gradually building on your knowledge. Each chapter is packed with practical information, code examples, and explanations to make it easy to understand and apply these concepts in your own projects.

Invitation to Read

So, are you ready to unlock the true power of Elixir? Let's embark on this exciting journey together! This book is your key to building high-performance backend systems that are fast, scalable, and ready to handle anything you throw at them. Grab a cup of coffee, settle in, and get ready to master the art of Elixir concurrency!

Chapter 1: Concurrency

We're about to unlock the secret sauce for building backend systems that are fast, responsive, and can handle anything you throw at them. In this first chapter, we'll crack open the concept of concurrency, explore how Elixir uses it like a boss, and finally, unveil the incredible benefits it brings to your backend projects. Let's dive in!

1.1 Concurrency:

In the realm of backend development, where responsiveness and efficiency reign supreme, concurrency emerges as a powerful tool. But what exactly is concurrency, and how can it benefit your backend systems? This section provides a clear and concise explanation, making it accessible for both beginners and experienced developers.

What is Concurrency?

Concurrency refers to a program's ability to handle multiple tasks (or requests) at the same time. Imagine a web server processing user requests. Traditionally, a single-threaded approach would handle each request sequentially, meaning one request must finish before the next can begin. This can lead to bottlenecks and slow response times, especially under high traffic.

Concurrency in Action: The Multitasking Advantage

Concurrency breaks free from this limitation. By utilizing multiple threads or processes, the server can handle multiple user requests simultaneously. Think of it like a busy restaurant kitchen. While one chef grills steaks, another prepares vegetables, and a third assembles desserts. All tasks progress concurrently, ensuring a smooth and efficient operation.

Benefits of Concurrency for Backend Systems

Now that we understand the core concept, let's explore the practical benefits concurrency brings to backend systems:

- **Enhanced Responsiveness:** With concurrency, users don't have to wait for one request to finish before another starts. This leads to a significant improvement in perceived responsiveness, especially for applications handling frequent user interactions.
- **Improved Scalability:** As your user base grows, your backend system needs to keep up. Concurrency allows you to scale horizontally by adding more processing power (like adding more chefs to the kitchen). This ensures your system can handle increasing workloads without sacrificing performance.
- **Efficient Resource Utilization:** Traditional single-threaded applications often leave resources idle while waiting for tasks to complete. Concurrency helps utilize available resources more effectively by keeping multiple processes running simultaneously. This translates to better overall performance for your backend system.

In essence, concurrency empowers you to build backend systems that are:

- **Faster:** Handle user requests with greater speed and efficiency.
- **More Scalable:** Adapt to growing user bases and increased demands.
- **More Efficient:** Utilize system resources more effectively.

Unveiling Elixir's Approach to Concurrency

The concept of concurrency lays the foundation for building powerful backend systems. In the next section, we'll delve deeper into how Elixir, a powerful language specifically designed for concurrency, utilizes this concept to create exceptional backend applications. We'll explore the Erlang VM and the Actor Model, the cornerstones of Elixir's approach to concurrency.

1.2 Elixir's Concurrency Playground:

Elixir takes a unique and powerful approach to concurrency, built upon two key pillars: the Erlang Virtual Machine (VM) and the Actor Model. This section will unpack these concepts, explaining how they empower Elixir to excel in building concurrent backend systems.

The Erlang VM:

The Erlang VM is a virtual machine specifically designed for building applications that leverage concurrency. Unlike traditional VMs focused on single-threaded execution, the Erlang VM excels at managing lightweight processes. These processes, akin to miniaturized programs, operate independently and can communicate with each other.

Think of the Erlang VM as a well-equipped kitchen. It efficiently manages multiple chefs (processes) who work independently on their assigned tasks (handling requests). The VM provides the resources and infrastructure necessary for these processes to function smoothly and efficiently.

The Actor Model: Structured Communication for Concurrent Systems

The Actor Model is a concurrency paradigm that dictates how processes interact and coordinate. It treats each process as an "actor" with its own private state and message queue. Actors can only communicate with each other by sending and receiving messages, ensuring a well-defined and structured interaction pattern.

Imagine the chefs in our kitchen communicating solely through written notes. This structured approach prevents misunderstandings and ensures each chef focuses on their specific task while collaborating effectively.

Benefits of the Erlang VM and Actor Model in Elixir

By leveraging these two cornerstones, Elixir offers several advantages for building concurrent backend systems:

- **Isolation and Fault Tolerance:** Since processes are isolated, a failure in one process doesn't bring down the entire system. This inherent fault tolerance makes your backend system more reliable and resilient to errors.
- **Simplified Communication:** The Actor Model promotes clear and controlled communication between processes, reducing the risk of race

conditions (where multiple processes attempt to modify shared data concurrently). This leads to more maintainable and predictable concurrent code.

- **Efficient Resource Management:** The Erlang VM efficiently manages lightweight processes, allowing you to utilize system resources effectively. This translates to better overall performance for your backend system.

Exploring the Power of Concurrency in Elixir

We've now explored the foundation of Elixir's approach to concurrency. In the next section, we'll delve deeper into the practical aspects. We'll uncover specific tools and techniques Elixir provides to build robust and scalable backend systems that leverage the power of concurrency.

1.3 Benefits Galore:

We've established the core concepts of concurrency and how Elixir utilizes them with the Erlang VM and the Actor Model. Now, let's jump into the real-world benefits that concurrency brings to the table for your backend systems.

Handling the Traffic Surge: Concurrency as Your Scalability Superhero

Imagine a high-traffic event on your e-commerce website. A traditional single-threaded backend system might struggle to keep up, leading to slow response times and frustrated customers. This is where concurrency shines! By leveraging multiple processes, your backend can handle a surge in user requests simultaneously.

Think of it like a well-staffed restaurant during peak hours. With multiple servers taking orders and chefs preparing food in parallel, the kitchen can efficiently handle the increased load, ensuring a smooth dining experience for everyone.

The Power of Asynchronous Tasks: Keeping Your Backend Responsive

Many backend applications involve tasks that don't require immediate user interaction, such as sending emails, processing payments, or generating reports. Concurrency allows you to execute these tasks asynchronously, meaning they run in the background without impacting the responsiveness of the main application.

Imagine a user submitting an order on your e-commerce platform. While the confirmation page loads immediately, the order processing and payment verification can occur asynchronously as separate processes. This keeps the user interface responsive and prevents a delay in user experience.

Building Fault-Tolerant Systems: Concurrency as Your Backend's Guardian

A crucial benefit of concurrency is its inherent fault tolerance. Since processes in Elixir are isolated, a failure in one process doesn't necessarily bring down the entire system. This is because processes communicate through messages, and a failing process doesn't directly affect the functionality of others.

Think of it like a modular kitchen with independent stations. If the grill malfunctions, the other chefs can continue preparing side dishes and desserts. The overall operation might be slightly impacted, but the kitchen can still function and fulfill orders.

The Benefits Recap: Building Winning Backend Systems with Concurrency

In summary, concurrency empowers you to build backend systems that are:

- **Highly Scalable:** Efficiently handle increasing user loads without compromising performance.
- **Responsive:** Maintain a smooth user experience even while executing background tasks.
- **Fault-Tolerant:** Remain operational even if individual processes encounter errors.

Putting Concurrency into Action

Now that you understand the advantages of concurrency, you're ready to explore how Elixir leverages it in practical terms. The next chapter will unveil the building blocks of concurrency in Elixir, equipping you with the tools to construct robust and scalable backend systems. We'll explore concepts like processes, message passing, and supervision techniques, all designed to empower you to harness the power of concurrency in your Elixir projects.

Chapter 2: Building Blocks of Concurrency

We've explored the magic behind concurrency and how Elixir leverages it for building powerful backend systems. Now, it's time to roll up our sleeves and dive into the actual tools Elixir provides for building these marvels. Buckle up, because we're about to explore the essential building blocks of concurrency – processes, GenServer behaviors, and tasks!

2.1 Processes:

Let's explore the magic of concurrency and its potential to build high-performance backend systems. Now, let's delve into the heart of Elixir's approach to concurrency: processes. These are the fundamental building blocks that enable you to create applications that handle multiple tasks simultaneously.

What are Processes?

A process in Elixir is a lightweight unit of execution. Think of it as a miniature program that can run independently and concurrently with other processes. Unlike traditional threads found in other languages, processes are much more lightweight and require fewer resources. This allows you to create a large number of processes without overwhelming your system.

Here's an analogy to illustrate the concept: Imagine a busy restaurant kitchen. Each chef working independently on assigned tasks (grilling steaks, preparing vegetables, etc.) represents a process in Elixir. They operate concurrently, ensuring smooth and efficient meal preparation.

Key Characteristics of Processes

- **Lightweight:** Processes are designed to be resource-efficient, making them ideal for building scalable concurrent applications.
- **Isolated Execution:** Each process has its own memory space, preventing data conflicts. This ensures data integrity and simplifies debugging.
- **Concurrent Execution:** Multiple processes can run simultaneously, handling requests or tasks in parallel. This translates to faster execution times and a more responsive backend system.

Benefits of Using Processes

- **Improved Scalability:** By distributing workload across multiple processes, you can easily scale your backend system to handle increasing demands.
- **Enhanced Responsiveness:** Concurrent execution of processes allows your system to handle user requests more efficiently, leading to a faster and more responsive user experience.
- **Simplified Development:** Breaking down complex tasks into smaller, independent processes can make your code easier to understand, maintain, and test.

Example: A Simple Process in Elixir

Here's a basic example of a process in Elixir that prints a message to the console:

Elixir

```elixir
defmodule MyApp.GreetingProcess do

  def start_link(name) do

    {:ok, pid} = spawn(fn ->

      IO.puts "Hello from #{name}!"

    end)

    {:ok, pid}

  end

end
```

In this example:

- We define a module named **MyApp.GreetingProcess**.
- The **start_link/1** function takes a **name** argument and creates a new process using the **spawn/1** function.
- The anonymous function passed to **spawn** prints a greeting message to the console using the provided **name**.

Processes are the foundation of concurrency in Elixir. Their lightweight nature, isolated execution, and ability to run concurrently make them ideal for building scalable and responsive backend systems. In the next section, we'll explore how to manage state within processes using GenServer behaviors, another crucial building block for robust concurrent applications.

2.2 Managing State with GenServer Behaviors:

Processes, the tiny powerhouses of concurrency we explored in the previous section, are fantastic for handling independent tasks. But what about situations where processes need to manage and access shared state? This is where GenServer behaviors come in – the ultimate organizers for state management in Elixir's concurrent world.

What are GenServer Behaviors?

A GenServer behavior is a special type of process specifically designed for managing state in a structured and reliable way. It acts as a central hub for data access and manipulation within your concurrent application. Imagine a well-organized kitchen with a designated area (the GenServer) for storing ingredients (the state) and a clear system for chefs (other processes) to request and use them.

Key Features of GenServer Behaviors

- **Structured Communication:** GenServer behaviors define clear protocols for how processes interact and exchange information. Processes can send messages to the GenServer requesting specific data or actions, ensuring controlled and predictable state changes.
- **State Management:** GenServer behaviors encapsulate the state of your application. Processes don't have direct access to the state; they must interact with the GenServer to modify or retrieve data. This prevents accidental data corruption and simplifies debugging.

- **Supervision:** GenServer behaviors can be supervised by other processes. This means if a GenServer crashes, the supervisor can restart it, ensuring the overall system remains operational. Think of a head chef overseeing the ingredient area – if something goes wrong with the GenServer (ingredient storage), the supervisor can intervene and get things back on track.

Benefits of Using GenServer Behaviors

- **Improved Data Consistency:** By centralizing state management, GenServer behaviors prevent data conflicts and ensure all processes have access to the same, up-to-date data.
- **Simplified Development:** Clear separation between process logic and state management leads to cleaner and more maintainable code. Debugging becomes easier as you can pinpoint state-related issues within the GenServer.
- **Enhanced Fault Tolerance:** Supervision capabilities of GenServer behaviors allow your system to recover from errors gracefully, ensuring continuous operation.

Example: A Simple GenServer Behavior

Let's create a basic GenServer behavior that keeps track of a counter:

Elixir

```elixir
defmodule MyApp.CounterServer do
```

```elixir
use GenServer

def init(initial_value) do
  {:ok, initial_value}
end

def handle_call({:increment}, _from, count) do
  {:reply, count + 1, count + 1}
end


def handle_call({:get}, _from, count) do
  {:reply, count, count}
end


defp handle_cast({:increment}, count) do
  {:noreply, count + 1}
end
end
```

Here's a breakdown of the code:

- We define a module named MyApp.CounterServer that utilizes the GenServer behavior.

- The init/1 function initializes the GenServer with an initial counter value.
- The **handle_call/3** function defines how the GenServer responds to incoming calls (requests from other processes). In this case, we handle two types of calls:
    - **{:increment}**: Increments the counter value and sends a reply with the new value.
    - *{:get}*: Returns the current counter value without modifying it.
- The **handle_cast/2** function (optional) defines how the GenServer responds to incoming casts (messages intended for side effects). Here, we simply increment the counter value without sending a reply.

Using the GenServer Behavior

Now, let's see how other processes can interact with our **CounterServer**:

Elixir

```elixir
defmodule MyApp.ProcessA do

 def start_link do

  GenServer.start_link(MyApp.CounterServer, 0)

 end

 def increment(pid) do

  GenServer.call(pid, {:increment})

 end
```

```
def get_count(pid) do

  GenServer.call(pid, {:get})

end

end
```

This code defines a module named **MyApp.ProcessA** that interacts with the **CounterServer**:

- The **start_link/0** function starts a new **CounterServer** process.
- The **increment/1** function sends a **{:increment}** call to the server, requesting to increase the counter value.
- The **get_count/1** function sends a **{:get}** call to the server, requesting the current counter value.

GenServer behaviors are essential tools for managing state in Elixir's concurrent applications. They provide structured communication, centralized state management, and supervision capabilities, leading to robust and maintainable systems.

2.3 Tasks: Single-Use Processes for Asynchronous Work

In the world of concurrency, not all tasks are created equal. Sometimes, you need processes to handle specific, one-time jobs that don't require immediate results. Enter tasks – the nimble assistants in Elixir's concurrency toolbox!

What are Tasks?

Tasks are essentially single-use processes designed for asynchronous work. Think of them as the kitchen runners in a busy restaurant. They handle specific, non-critical tasks like delivering food to tables or notifying the waitstaff about completed orders. Once their job is done, they're free to move on to the next task, ensuring a smooth flow in the kitchen.

Key Characteristics of Tasks

- **Single-Use:** Unlike traditional processes that can handle multiple requests, tasks are designed to execute a single unit of work. Once the work is complete, the task terminates.
- **Asynchronous Execution:** Tasks run concurrently with your main application, freeing up your main processes to handle user requests or other tasks. This improves responsiveness and prevents delays in the overall system.
- **Lightweight:** Similar to processes, tasks are lightweight and resource-efficient, making them ideal for handling a large number of asynchronous jobs.

Benefits of Using Tasks

- **Improved Responsiveness:** By offloading non-critical work to asynchronous tasks, you prevent your main processes from getting bogged down, leading to a more responsive user experience.

- **Enhanced Scalability:** Tasks allow you to easily scale your application to handle increasing workloads by distributing asynchronous jobs across multiple resources.
- **Simplified Code:** Separating asynchronous work into dedicated tasks can improve code readability and maintainability.

Example: A Simple Task for Sending an Email

Let's see how to create a task in Elixir to send a confirmation email after a user signs up:

Elixir

```elixir
defmodule MyApp.EmailTask do

 def send_confirmation_email(email) do

  Task.start_link(fn ->

   IO.puts "Sending confirmation email to #{email}"

    # Simulate email sending process (replace with actual email sending logic)

   Process.sleep(1000)

  end)

 end

end
```

Here's a breakdown of the code:

- We define a module named **MyApp.EmailTask**.
- The **send_confirmation_email/1** function takes an email address as input.
- The function uses **Task.start_link/1** to create a new task. The anonymous function passed to **start_link** defines the work the task will perform:
  - It prints a message indicating the email is being sent.
  - It simulates the email sending process with a sleep (replace this with your actual email sending logic).

Using the Email Task

Now, let's integrate this task into our user sign-up process:

Elixir

```elixir
defmodule MyApp.SignupController do

  def create(conn, %{"user" => user_params}) do

    # ... (user creation logic) ...


    MyApp.EmailTask.send_confirmation_email(user_params["email"])

    conn |> put_flash(:info, "User created successfully!") |> redirect(...)

  end

end
```

In this example:

- The **SignupController.create/2** function handles user sign-up requests.
- After creating the user, it calls the **send_confirmation_email/1** function to send an email asynchronously.
- The user creation process continues without waiting for the email to be sent.

Tasks are a powerful tool for handling asynchronous work in Elixir. They improve responsiveness, enhance scalability, and simplify your code by separating concerns. In the next chapter, we'll delve deeper into the world of messaging and supervision, the glue that holds your concurrent applications together!

Chapter 3: Messaging and Supervision

We've explored lore the building blocks of concurrency in Elixir – processes, GenServer behaviors, and tasks. Now, it's time to move into the communication channels and safety nets that keep your concurrent applications running smoothly: messaging and supervision!

3.1 Message Passing:

Here we will focus on building blocks of concurrency in Elixir: processes, GenServer behaviors, and tasks. Now, let's delve into the communication channels that keep these processes working together – message passing! It's the essential language that allows processes to exchange information, coordinate tasks, and ultimately make your entire concurrent application function smoothly.

Imagine a busy airport. Different departments like security, baggage claim, and gate staff all need to communicate effectively to ensure a smooth passenger experience. This communication can be seen as a message passing in Elixir. Processes act like these departments, and messages are the information they exchange.

Here's a breakdown of the key aspects of message passing in Elixir:

- **Structured Communication:** Unlike shouting across a crowded room, processes send messages with a clear structure. This structure typically includes:
  - **Data:** The actual information being sent, like weather data or a passenger's boarding pass.
  - **Message Type:** A label that identifies the type of information being sent, like "weather_update" or "boarding_pass_request". This helps the receiving process understand how to handle the message.
- **Asynchronous Delivery:** Processes don't wait for a reply before continuing with their work. This keeps them independent and efficient. Think of a security officer scanning a passport – they don't wait for confirmation from baggage claim before moving on to the next passenger.
- **Flexibility:** Processes can handle different types of messages, allowing for versatile communication patterns. Just like the airport staff can handle various requests from passengers, processes can adapt to different message types.

Benefits of Message Passing

- **Decoupled Processes:** Processes don't need to be aware of each other's internal workings. They simply send and receive messages, making development and maintenance easier. Imagine the security officer doesn't need to know the entire baggage claim process – they just need to know how to scan passports and send relevant information (messages) about the passenger.

- **Error Handling:** Messages can be used to signal errors or request retries, leading to more robust applications. If the security scanner malfunctions, it can send an error message to a maintenance process for repair.
- **Scalability:** Messaging allows for easy scaling by adding more processes without affecting communication patterns. As passenger volume increases, you can add more security officers without changing how they communicate with other airport staff.

Example: Sending Weather Updates with Messages

Let's see how message passing can be used in practice:

Elixir

```elixir
defmodule MyApp.WeatherFetcher do

 def fetch_weather(location) do

    # Simulate fetching weather data (replace with actual logic)

   weather_data = %{city: location, temperature: 25}

      send(MyApp.WeatherDisplay, {:weather_update, location, weather_data})

 end

end
```

```
defmodule MyApp.WeatherDisplay do

    def handle_cast({:weather_update, location, data},
_state) do

          IO.puts "Current weather in #{location}:
#{data.temperature}°C"

 end

end
```

In this example:

- The **WeatherFetcher** process retrieves weather data and sends a message containing the location and data to the **WeatherDisplay** process using . This message is like a weather report being sent from the weather service to a news station.
- The **WeatherDisplay** process receives the message using the handle_cast/2 callback and displays the weather information just like a news station might broadcast the weather report.

By using messages, the **WeatherFetcher** and **WeatherDisplay** processes can communicate effectively without needing to know each other's internal details. This makes the code more modular and easier to maintain.

Example: Order Processing with Messages

Let's see how message passing can be used in an online store scenario:

defmodule MyApp.OrderPlacer do

```
def place_order(customer_id, items) do

  # Simulate order creation (replace with actual logic)

  order_id = generate_order_id()

      send(MyApp.OrderProcessor,   {:process_order,
order_id, customer_id, items})

  end

end

defmodule MyApp.OrderProcessor do

      def    handle_cast({:process_order,    order_id,
customer_id, items}, _state) do

  deduct_inventory(items)

      send(MyApp.InventoryManager,   {:update_stock,
items})

  # ... other order processing tasks ...

  end

end
```

In this example:

- The OrderPlacer process creates an order and sends a
  message containing the order details (order ID,
  customer ID, and items) to the OrderProcessor
  process using send/2. This message is like an order

confirmation being sent from the customer to the online store.

- The OrderProcessor process receives the message using the handle_cast/2 callback and performs various tasks like deducting inventory and updating stock levels. It might also send another message to the InventoryManager process to reflect the changes.

By using messages, the different departments (processes) in the online store can communicate and coordinate order processing efficiently without needing to be tightly coupled.

3.2 Building Fault Tolerance with Supervision Trees:

Imagine a bustling city with a complex network of power lines. Even in the best-maintained systems, occasional outages can occur. But what if a single power outage could plunge the entire city into darkness? Not ideal! This is where robust infrastructure steps in, ensuring localized failures don't bring down the whole system.

In the world of Elixir concurrency, supervision trees play a similar role. They act as the guardians of your application, ensuring it remains operational even when individual processes encounter errors. Let's explore how supervision trees achieve this feat.

What are Supervision Trees?

A supervision tree is a hierarchical structure that defines how your application handles process failures. It's like an organizational chart, with a supervisor process at the root overseeing its child processes. These child processes can themselves have child processes, forming a branching structure.

The Role of the Supervisor

The supervisor plays a critical role in the supervision tree. When a child process crashes, the supervisor takes action based on a pre-defined strategy. Here are some common strategies:

- **Restart:** The supervisor restarts the failed child process, essentially giving it a fresh start. This is ideal for situations where errors might be transient and the process can potentially recover.
- **Terminate:** The supervisor terminates the failed child process and potentially its entire subtree. This might be necessary for processes that can't recover from errors or if their failure could corrupt data.
- **Escalate:** The supervisor can escalate the error to its own supervisor, potentially triggering a chain of restarts or terminations depending on the overall tree structure and strategy.

Benefits of Supervision Trees

- **Improved System Availability:** By restarting failed processes, supervision trees ensure your application remains operational even if individual processes encounter errors. Imagine a single power line outage only affecting a specific neighborhood, not the entire city.

- **Isolation of Failures:** Errors are contained within failed processes, preventing them from cascading and bringing down the entire system. This is like a faulty traffic light at one intersection not causing gridlock in the entire city.
- **Simplified Error Handling:** Supervision trees automate process restarts or termination based on the chosen strategy, reducing the need for manual intervention. Think of automated backup generators kicking in to restore power during an outage.

Example: A Simple Supervision Tree

Here's a basic example of a supervision tree with a supervisor and two child processes:

Elixir

```elixir
defmodule MyApp.Supervisor do

  use Supervisor

  def init(_) do

    children = [

      worker(MyApp.WorkerA, []),

      worker(MyApp.WorkerB, [])

    ]

    {:ok, children, strategy: :one_for_one}
```

```
  end

end
```

This code defines a supervisor named **MyApp.Supervisor** with two child processes: **MyApp.WorkerA** and **MyApp.WorkerB**. The **strategy: :one_for_one** option indicates that the supervisor will only restart the specific child process that crashes, keeping the others running. This is like isolating a power outage to a specific neighborhood.

Supervision trees are a crucial concept in building robust and fault-tolerant Elixir applications. By defining clear supervision strategies, you ensure your application can gracefully handle process failures and maintain overall system availability. In the next section, we'll delve deeper into different supervision strategies and how to choose the right one for your specific needs.

3.3 Supervisor Strategies:

In the previous section, we explored supervision trees – the guardians of your Elixir application. We saw how they ensure system availability by overseeing child processes and taking action when failures occur. But the question remains: what kind of action should the supervisor take? This is where supervisor strategies come in – your toolbox for handling process failures.

Understanding Supervisor Strategies

Supervisor strategies define how a supervisor reacts when a child process crashes. These strategies offer different approaches to recovery, allowing you to tailor fault tolerance to your specific application needs. Here are the three most common strategies:

1. **:one_for_one:** This strategy, often considered the default, focuses on isolated recovery. When a child process fails, only that specific process is restarted. The supervisor leaves its healthy siblings untouched.

Imagine a multi-lane highway. If there's an accident in one lane, the traffic in that lane comes to a halt. However, traffic continues to flow normally in the other lanes. This is similar to the :one_for_one strategy, where a failing child process doesn't affect its healthy counterparts.

Code Example:

Elixir

```elixir
defmodule MyApp.Supervisor do

  use Supervisor


  def init(_) do

    children = [

      worker(MyApp.WorkerA, []),

      worker(MyApp.WorkerB, [])

    ]
```

```
{:ok, children, strategy: :one_for_one}

  end

end
```

2. :all_for_one: This strategy takes a more drastic approach. If any child process crashes, the entire supervision tree is terminated. This can be useful for situations where a single failure might compromise the integrity of the entire system, or if restarting a single process wouldn't be enough to recover from the error.

Think of a power grid. If a critical component fails, it can cause a cascading outage across the entire grid, affecting all connected systems. This is analogous to the :all_for_one strategy, where a single child process failure brings down the entire tree.

Code Example:

Elixir

```
defmodule MyApp.Supervisor do

  use Supervisor

  def init(_) do

    children = [

      worker(MyApp.WorkerA, []),

      worker(MyApp.WorkerB, [])
```

```
    ]
    {:ok, children, strategy: :all_for_one}

  end

end
```

3. **:one_for_one with Options:** The :one_for_one strategy can be further customized with additional options. Here are two commonly used options:
   o **:restart_intensity:** This option allows you to specify the maximum number of restart attempts before the supervisor gives up and terminates the process. It helps prevent infinite restarts in case of unrecoverable errors.
   o **:delay:** This option introduces a delay between restart attempts. This can be useful for situations where retrying immediately might overload the system or exacerbate the issue.

Choosing the Right Strategy

The best supervisor strategy depends on your application's specific needs. Here are some factors to consider:

- **Severity of errors:** If errors are typically transient and recoverable, :one_for_one might be sufficient. For critical errors that compromise data integrity, :all_for_one might be necessary.
- **Process dependencies:** If child processes heavily depend on each other, restarting one might require restarting others as well. In such cases,

:one_for_one with a short delay for dependent processes might be a good fit.

- **External dependencies**: If your application interacts with external resources, consider how failures in those resources might affect your processes.

Remember, there's no one-size-fits-all solution. Experiment with different strategies and tailor them to your application's specific requirements.

Supervisor strategies are an essential aspect of building robust and fault-tolerant Elixir applications. By understanding these strategies and choosing the right one for your needs, you ensure your application can gracefully handle process failures and maintain overall system availability.

Chapter 4: OTP Behaviours

We've explored the essential tools for communication and fault tolerance: message passing and supervision trees. Now, we're diving deeper into the world of OTP behaviours – the pre-built Lego blocks of Elixir for constructing robust and scalable concurrent applications.

4.1 Core OTP Behaviours:

We're stepping into the exciting world of OTP behaviours – pre-built modules that provide essential functionalities for structured concurrent programming. These behaviours act as the foundation for building robust and scalable Elixir applications.

Think of OTP behaviours like a well-equipped toolbox. Each tool has a specific purpose, and together they empower you to construct complex systems efficiently. Here, we'll meet the three core OTP behaviours:

1. **GenServer:** The **"State Management Maestro"**
   - A GenServer is a versatile process that excels at managing state and handling incoming messages. It acts as a central point of control for other processes, coordinating interactions and ensuring everything runs smoothly.
   - Imagine a GenServer as a state management maestro in an orchestra. It keeps track of the musical piece (state), receives instructions from the conductor (messages), and

coordinates the different instruments (processes) to play their parts in harmony.

Code Example (Simple GenServer):

Elixir

```elixir
defmodule Counter do

  use GenServer


  def init(initial_value) do

    {:ok, initial_value}

  end

  def handle_cast({:increment}, count) do

    {:noreply, count + 1}

  end

  def handle_info(_msg, count) do

    {:noreply, count}

  end

end
```

In this example, the Counter GenServer manages an integer state (the count). It can receive messages like {:increment} to increase the count and keeps track of the current value.

2. **Supervisor:** The "**Guardian Angel**"
    - We briefly encountered supervisors in Chapter 3. They act as the guardians of your application, overseeing child processes. If a child process crashes, the supervisor takes action, typically restarting it to ensure continued operation.
    - Supervisors are like guardian angels in your system, watching over child processes and making sure they stay healthy. If a process encounters an error and crashes, the supervisor can revive it, preventing cascading failures and system outages.

Code Example (Basic Supervisor):

Elixir

```elixir
defmodule MyApp.Supervisor do

  use Supervisor

  def init(_) do

    children = [

      worker(MyApp.WorkerA, [])

    ]

    {:ok, children, strategy: :one_for_one}

  end

end
```

This supervisor oversees a child process **MyApp.WorkerA**. If **WorkerA** crashes, the supervisor will typically restart it using the :**one_for_one** strategy.

3. **GenericPool: The "Resource Manager"**
   - Some tasks require resources like database connections or network sockets. The GenericPool behaviour helps you manage a pool of these resources efficiently. Processes can request resources from the pool when needed and return them when finished.
   - Think of a GenericPool as a resource manager at a resort. It manages a pool of lounge chairs (resources) – guests (processes) can request a chair when they arrive and return it when they leave. This ensures efficient allocation and prevents resource exhaustion.

Code Example (Simple Pool with GenServer):

Elixir

```
defmodule ConnectionPool do

  use GenServer


  def init(opts) do

    {:ok, Poolboy.start_link(opts)}

  end
```

```
def handle_cast({:request_connection}, state) do

  {:noreply, {:deliver, Poolboy.acquire(state)}}

end

# ... (other message handling functions)

end
```

This example uses a GenServer to manage a pool created by the **Poolboy** library. Processes can send a {:request_connection} message to acquire a connection from the pool.

These three core OTP behaviours – GenServer, Supervisor, and GenericPool – provide the foundation for building structured and robust concurrent applications in Elixir. By leveraging their functionalities, you can achieve efficient state management, reliable process supervision, and optimal resource utilization. In the next section, we'll explore how these behaviours work together to create well-organized concurrent systems.

4.2 Building Structured Concurrent Applications with OTP Behaviours:

Imagine a bustling city with various departments working together – the transportation department manages traffic flow, the power grid ensures consistent electricity, and the sanitation department keeps the streets clean. Each department has a specific role, yet they all contribute to the smooth operation of the entire city.

In the world of Elixir concurrency, OTP behaviours play a similar role. They provide a structured approach to building concurrent applications, where processes collaborate efficiently to achieve a common goal. Let's see how these behaviours work together:

1. Defining Responsibilities with GenServers:

- GenServers excel at managing state and handling messages. They act as central points of control for specific functionalities within your application.
- Think of each GenServer as a department head in our city analogy. The transportation department GenServer manages traffic flow (state) and receives messages about accidents or road closures.

Code Example (Simple Inventory GenServer):

Elixir

```elixir
defmodule Inventory do

  use GenServer

  def init(initial_stock) do

    {:ok, initial_stock}

  end

  def handle_cast({:add_item, item}, stock) do

    {:noreply, stock ++ [item]}
```

```
  end

  def handle_call({:get_stock}, _from, stock) do

    {:reply, stock, stock}

  end

end
```

This **Inventory** GenServer manages the current stock (state) as a list of items. It can receive messages to add new items and respond to calls to retrieve the current stock level.

2. Ensuring Process Health with Supervisors:

- Supervisors, as we saw earlier, act as guardians, overseeing child processes. They ensure these processes remain operational by restarting them if they encounter errors.
- Imagine the city having a central monitoring system (supervisor) that checks on all departments (child processes). If a department malfunctions (process crashes), the supervisor can restart it (process restart) to ensure continued service.

Code Example (Supervisor with Inventory GenServer):

Elixir

```
defmodule MyApp.Supervisor do

  use Supervisor

  def init(_) do
```

```
children = [

    worker(MyApp.InventoryServer, [100])  # Initial stock
of 100 items

  ]

  {:ok, children, strategy: :one_for_one}

end

end
```

This supervisor oversees the **MyApp.InventoryServer** GenServer. If the GenServer crashes, the supervisor will typically restart it using the :one_for_one strategy.

3. Efficient Resource Management with GenericPool:

- Some tasks require limited resources like database connections or network sockets. The GenericPool behaviour helps manage a pool of these resources, allowing processes to request and return them efficiently.
- Think of the city having a pool of shared vehicles (resources) used by different departments (processes). The sanitation department can request a vehicle to collect garbage, and when finished, return it to the pool for others to use.

Code Example (Simplified Pool with Function):

Elixir

```
def get_database_connection do
```

```
  Poolboy.acquire(connection_pool)

end

def release_database_connection(connection) do

  Poolboy.release(connection)

end
```

This example uses the **Poolboy** library to manage a pool of database connections. Processes can call **get_database_connection** to acquire a connection and **release_database_connection** to return it to the pool.

Benefits of Structured Concurrency:

- **Modular Design:** By using GenServers for specific tasks, you create a modular application structure, making it easier to understand, maintain, and test individual components.
- **Improved Fault Tolerance:** Supervisors ensure processes remain operational, preventing failures from cascading and impacting the entire system.
- **Efficient Resource Utilization:** GenericPool helps manage resource usage effectively, preventing bottlenecks and improving overall application performance.

In essence, OTP behaviours provide a well-defined approach to building concurrent applications. By leveraging their functionalities, you can create robust, scalable, and maintainable systems that excel in handling complex tasks with high efficiency.

4.3 Practical Examples of OTP Behaviours in Backend Systems:

Now that we understand the core OTP behaviours – GenServer, Supervisor, and GenericPool – let's see them in action with some practical examples commonly found in backend systems:

1. Chat Application:

Imagine building a real-time chat application. Here's how OTP behaviours can be used:

- **GenServer:** A Chatroom GenServer can manage the state of each chat room, storing messages and user information. It can handle messages to add new messages, retrieve message history, and manage user connections.
- **Supervisor:** A supervisor can oversee child processes like the Chatroom GenServer and other processes responsible for user authentication and message broadcasting.
- **GenericPool (Optional):** If the application uses external services like a message queue for broadcasting messages, a GenericPool might manage connections to that service.

Code Example (Simplified Chatroom GenServer):

Elixir

```
defmodule Chatroom do
```

```elixir
use GenServer

def init(room_name) do
  {:ok, %{name: room_name, messages: []}}
end

def handle_cast({:new_message, user, message}, state) do
  updated_messages = state.messages ++ [{user: user, message: message}]

  {:noreply, %{state | messages: updated_messages}}
end

# ... (other message handling functions for user joining/leaving, etc.)
end
```

2. E-commerce Platform:

Building an e-commerce platform involves managing products, orders, and payments. OTP behaviours can be instrumental here:

- **GenServer:** Separate GenServers can manage product catalogs, shopping carts, and user accounts. They can handle messages to add/update products, add/remove items from carts, and process user information.

- **Supervisor:** A supervisor can oversee these GenServers and other child processes responsible for tasks like order processing and payment gateway integration.
- **GenericPool:** A GenericPool might manage database connections for product information and order details.

Code Example (Simplified Product GenServer):

Elixir

```elixir
defmodule Product do

  use GenServer


  def init(initial_data) do

    {:ok, initial_data}

  end

      def handle_cast({:update_stock, new_stock}, product_data) do

    {:noreply, %{product_data | stock: new_stock}}

  end

  # ... (other message handling functions for product details retrieval, etc.)

end
```

3. Background Processing System:

Many backend systems require background tasks like sending emails, processing payments asynchronously, or generating reports. OTP behaviours can be used for:

- **GenServer:** A background job queue GenServer can manage a list of tasks to be processed. It can receive messages to enqueue new jobs and handle worker processes that complete tasks.
- **Supervisor:** A supervisor can oversee child worker processes that dequeue and execute jobs from the queue.
- **GenericPool (Optional):** If background tasks involve external interactions like sending emails, a GenericPool might manage connections to those services.

Code Example (Simplified Job Queue GenServer):

Elixir

```
defmodule JobQueue do

  use GenServer


  def init(initial_jobs) do

   {:ok, initial_jobs}

  end
```

```elixir
def handle_cast({:enqueue_job, job}, jobs) do

  {:noreply, jobs ++ [job]}

end

# ... (other message handling functions for job retrieval
and worker supervision)

end
```

These are just a few examples, and the possibilities are vast! By leveraging OTP behaviours effectively, you can build robust, scalable, and maintainable backend systems capable of handling complex functionalities and high traffic.

In the next chapter, we'll delve deeper into advanced techniques for using OTP behaviours and explore how to leverage them for even more powerful concurrent applications.

Chapter 5: Channels and Agents for Advanced Coordination:

In the previous chapter, we explored the power of OTP behaviours for building structured concurrent applications. Now, we're venturing into more advanced territory – Channels and Agents. These tools provide even more sophisticated mechanisms for coordinating processes and exchanging data efficiently.

5.1 Efficient Data Exchange with Channels:

In the world of Elixir concurrency, efficient data exchange between processes is crucial. While GenServers provide a robust mechanism for message passing, channels offer a more streamlined approach specifically designed for high-performance data exchange.

Understanding Channels:

- Channels are lightweight, unidirectional conduits for sending and receiving data between processes. Unlike GenServers, which handle back-and-forth message exchanges, channels offer a more focused approach for data flow.

Think of it this way: Imagine a factory assembly line. Processes act as different stations, and channels are the conveyor belts that carry parts (data) between them. Each station performs its specific task on the data as it moves along the channel.

Benefits of Channels:

- **Efficiency:** Channels are optimized for data exchange, leading to faster communication compared to GenServer messages.
- **Scalability:** Channels can handle large volumes of data efficiently, making them suitable for high-traffic applications.
- **Simplicity:** Channels offer a simpler approach for data flow compared to the message-oriented communication of GenServers.

Key Concepts:

- **Sending Data (Writing to a Channel):** The Channel.send(channel, data) function is used to send data (the part) onto a specific channel (the conveyor belt).
- **Receiving Data (Reading from a Channel):** The Channel.receive(channel) function is used by a process to receive data (pick up the part) from the channel. It waits until data is available or times out after a specified period.

Code Example (Simple Data Exchange with a Channel):

Elixir

```
defmodule Producer do

  def start(channel) do
```

```elixir
  spawn(fn ->

    Enum.each(1..10, fn(item) ->

        Channel.send(channel, item)  # Send each item (1 to 10) to the channel

        Process.sleep(100)  # Simulate some work between sending items

      end)

    end)

    end

  end
end

defmodule Consumer do

  def start(channel) do

    spawn(fn ->

      receive do

        data -> IO.inspect(data)  # Inspect the received data (item)

      end

      loop

    end)

  end
```

end

channel = Channel.new() # Create a new channel

Producer.start(channel) # Start the producer process

Consumer.start(channel) # Start the consumer process

In this example, the **Producer** process sends numbers (1 to 10) one by one onto the channel using **Channel.send**. The **Consumer** process waits on the channel using **Channel.receive** and inspects each received item (number).

Choosing Between Channels and GenServers:

- Use channels when you need a high-performance, unidirectional flow of data between processes.
- Use GenServers when you need more complex message-based communication, state management, or handling replies from processes.

By understanding channels and their advantages, you can streamline communication between processes in your Elixir applications, leading to improved performance and scalability.

5.2 Managing Mutable Shared State with Agents and Supervision:

In the exciting world of Elixir concurrency, managing mutable shared state (data that can be changed) effectively is crucial. While channels excel at data exchange, they're not ideal for state management. Here's where Agents come in, along with their trusty companion, Supervision.

Understanding Agents:

- **Agents:** Agents are special processes that encapsulate mutable shared state. They provide a safe and controlled way for multiple processes to access and update this state concurrently. Think of an Agent as a secure vault where processes can enter with proper authorization (functions) to access or modify valuables (state) stored inside.

The Challenge of Mutable Shared State:

Imagine multiple people trying to edit the same document simultaneously without proper coordination. Chaos ensues! Similarly, in concurrent programming, uncoordinated access to shared state can lead to unexpected behavior and errors.

Agents to the Rescue:

Agents act as gatekeepers for shared state. Processes cannot directly modify the state; they interact with Agents using functions provided by the Agent. These functions ensure that updates are applied atomically (all or nothing at once), preventing inconsistencies.

Supervision: The Guardian of Agents:

Agents are powerful, but they require careful handling. Since they hold mutable state, errors during updates can lead to problems. This is where Supervision comes into play.

Supervision in Action:

- Supervisors can be configured to oversee Agents. If an error occurs during an Agent update, the supervisor can restart the Agent. This ensures the Agent's state remains consistent and prevents cascading errors in your application.
- Think of the Agent's vault having a supervisor (guard) who monitors activity. If someone tries to tamper with the valuables (causing an error), the guard can reset the vault (restart the Agent) to prevent inconsistencies.

Code Example (Simple Counter with Agent and Supervisor):

Elixir

```
defmodule CounterAgent do

  use Agent

  def init(initial_value) do

    {:ok, initial_value}

  end

  def get(state) do

    state

  end
```

```elixir
  def increment(state) do

    {:ok, state + 1}

  end

end

defmodule CounterSupervisor do

  use Supervisor

  def init(_) do

    children = [

      worker(CounterAgent, [0])

    ]

    {:ok, children, strategy: :one_for_one}

  end

end
```

In this example, an Agent manages the counter state (initially 0). The **increment** function, provided by the Agent, updates the state atomically. The supervisor oversees the Agent, ensuring its continued operation and restarting it if necessary.

Remember:

- Use Agents for managing mutable shared state that needs concurrent access.

- Leverage Supervision to ensure Agent state consistency and application stability.

By understanding Agents and Supervision, you can effectively manage mutable shared state in your Elixir applications, leading to robust and reliable concurrent systems.

5.3 Advanced Techniques for Coordinating Processes with Channels and Agents:

Channels and Agents, combined with OTP behaviours and supervision, unlock a vast toolkit for building sophisticated concurrent applications in Elixir. Here, we'll explore some exciting techniques to take your process coordination skills to the next level.

1. Building Fault-Tolerant Pipelines

Imagine an assembly line where parts (data) are processed by different stations (processes). What happens if a machine malfunctions? In concurrent programming, errors can disrupt data pipelines. Channels can help build fault-tolerant pipelines:

- **Concept:** Processes send data through a chain of channels. Each channel connects one process to the next, forming a pipeline.
- **Fault Tolerance:** Supervisors can oversee processes in the pipeline. If a process crashes, the supervisor can

restart it, ensuring data keeps flowing after a brief interruption.

Code Example (Simple Fault–Tolerant Pipeline with Channels and Supervision):

Elixir

```elixir
defmodule DataFormatter do

  def start(channel_in, channel_out) do

    spawn(fn ->

      receive do

        data ->

          formatted_data = format_data(data)

          Channel.send(channel_out, formatted_data)

        after

          1000 -> :timeout

      end

      loop

    end)

  end

end

defmodule DataValidator do
```

```
def start(channel__in) do

  spawn(fn ->

    receive do

      data ->

        if valid?(data) do

          IO.inspect(data)

        end

      after

        1000 -> :timeout

    end

    loop

  end)

end

end
```

... (Supervisor definition overseeing DataFormatter and DataValidator)

channel1 = Channel.new()

channel2 = Channel.new()

DataFormatter.start(channel1, channel2)

```elixir
DataValidator.start(channel2)

# Simulate sending data

Enum.each(1..3, fn(i) ->

  Channel.send(channel1, "data#{i}")

  Process.sleep(200)

end)
```

In this example, a supervisor oversees two processes: **DataFormatter** and **DataValidator**. Data flows from **channel1** to **channel2** using channels. The supervisor ensures that if a process crashes, it's restarted, and the data pipeline remains functional.

2. Implementing Publish-Subscribe Patterns

Imagine a news platform where multiple reporters (processes) can publish updates (data). Editors (other processes) can subscribe to receive these updates efficiently. Channels enable a publish-subscribe pattern:

- **Concept:** A single channel acts as a publisher. Multiple processes can subscribe to this channel to receive published data.
- **Efficiency:** Processes only receive data they're interested in, reducing unnecessary processing.

Code Example (Publish-Subscribe with Channels):

Elixir

```elixir
defmodule NewsPublisher do

  def start(channel) do

    spawn(fn ->

      Enum.each(1..3, fn(i) ->

        Channel.cast(channel, "News update #{i}")

        Process.sleep(500)

      end)

    end)

  end

end


defmodule SportsEditor do

  def start(channel) do

    spawn(fn ->

      receive do

        message ->

          if String.starts_with?(message, "Sports news"), do:
IO.inspect(message)

        end

      end
```

```elixir
    end)

  end

end


defmodule WorldEditor do

  def start(channel) do

    spawn(fn ->

      receive do

        message ->

          if String.starts_with?(message, "World news"), do:
IO.inspect(message)

        end

      end

    end)

  end

end


channel = Channel.new()


NewsPublisher.start(channel)
```

SportsEditor.start(channel)

WorldEditor.start(channel)

In this example, a NewsPublisher broadcasts messages on a channel. The SportsEditor and WorldEditor processes subscribe to the channel and only receive messages that match their specific interests (sports or world news).

3. Coordinating Distributed Processes

Imagine a large-scale application running on multiple servers. Channels and Agents can be used to coordinate processes across these servers:

- **Concept:** Processes on different servers can communicate by sending messages through channels or accessing a shared Agent replicated across servers.
- **Distributed Coordination:** This enables complex interactions between processes even when they're physically separated.

Note: Implementing distributed coordination is an advanced topic and requires careful design and tooling considerations.

These are just a few examples of the many advanced techniques

Chapter 6: Tasking and Managing Asynchronous Work

We've explored the power of channels and agents for advanced process coordination. Now, we're diving into the exciting world of asynchronous tasks. Buckle up, because we're about to learn how to make your Elixir applications ninjas of handling work "in the background."

6.1 The Task Module and Task Supervisor for Asynchronous Workloads

In the fast-paced world of Elixir applications, handling tasks efficiently is crucial. While your main processes are busy handling user requests, there might be background jobs that don't require immediate attention. Enter the world of asynchronous tasks, where the Task module and Task.Supervisor become your trusted companions.

Understanding Asynchronous Tasks:

- **Asynchronous Tasks:** Imagine a restaurant with chefs (your main processes) preparing main courses. Chopping vegetables or baking bread (background tasks) can be done asynchronously by kitchen assistants (tasks). These tasks run concurrently with the main processes, improving overall efficiency.
- **Tasks vs Processes:** Both tasks and processes are units of execution in Elixir. However, tasks are lightweight and specifically designed for short-lived,

asynchronous operations. Unlike heavyweight processes with their own mailboxes, tasks share the mailbox of their parent process.

The Task Module:

- **Task.start(fun):** This function is the heart of asynchronous tasks in Elixir. It takes a function (fun) as an argument and starts its execution as a separate task. The main process continues executing without waiting for the task to finish.

Code Example (Simple Task for Sending an Email):

Elixir

```
def send_email(email_address, message) do

  Task.start(fn -> Email.deliver(email_address, message)
end)

end

# Calling the function from within your main process

send_email("user@example.com", "Your order has been
confirmed!")
```

In this example, the **send_email** function doesn't wait for the email to be delivered. It simply creates a task that handles sending the email asynchronously, freeing up the main process to continue serving other requests.

The Task.Supervisor:

- **Ensuring Task Order and Error Handling:** While tasks are great for asynchronous operations, sometimes you might need more control. The **Task.Supervisor** provides supervision for tasks, ensuring they are started in a specific order and restarted if they encounter errors.
- **Benefits of Task.Supervisor:**
  - **Ordered Execution:** You can define the order in which tasks are started, ensuring tasks that depend on others are executed in the correct sequence.
  - **Restart Strategy:** The supervisor can be configured to restart failed tasks, preventing your application from crashing due to a single task failure.

Code Example (Task.Supervisor with Ordered Execution):

Elixir

```
defmodule MyTasks do

  use Task.Supervisor

  def init(_) do

    children = [

        worker(fn -> send_email("user1@example.com", "Welcome!") end),

        worker(fn -> send_email("user2@example.com", "Welcome!") end)

    ]
```

```elixir
    {:ok, children, strategy: :one_for_one}

  end

end

MyTasks.start_link()
```

In this example, the **MyTasks** supervisor ensures that the emails are sent in the specified order (**user1** first, then **user2**). The **:one_for_one** strategy tells the supervisor to restart only the failing task if an error occurs.

Code Example (Simple Task for Sending an Email):

Elixir

```elixir
def send_email(email_address, message) do

  Task.start(fn -> Email.deliver(email_address, message) end)

end

# Calling the function from within your main process

send_email("user@example.com", "Your
```

Note:

- Asynchronous tasks are a powerful tool for improving application responsiveness.
- Use the **Task** module to easily create and run tasks concurrently.

- Leverage the Task.Supervisor for ordered execution, error handling, and robust task management.

By effectively utilizing tasks and supervision, you can build scalable and efficient Elixir applications that handle both immediate and background operations seamlessly.

6.2 Handling Task Failures and Ensuring Application Responsiveness:

In the world of Elixir applications, asynchronous tasks are your ninjas for handling background work. But even ninjas stumble sometimes! This section delves into how to handle task failures while keeping your application responsive and robust.

Understanding Task Failures:

- **Unexpected Errors:** Tasks can fail due to various reasons: network issues, database errors, bugs in the task's code, or even external service outages. It's essential to have mechanisms in place to catch these failures and prevent them from crashing your entire application.
- **Impact on Responsiveness:** Unhandled task failures can lead to unexpected behavior or even application crashes. By addressing failures, you ensure your application remains responsive to user requests, even when background tasks encounter issues.

Techniques for Handling Task Failures:

1. **Linking and Monitoring Tasks with GenServers:**
   - **Leveraging GenServers:** While linking tasks is helpful, GenServers offer a more structured approach. A GenServer can manage a pool of tasks, receive notifications about task failures, and potentially handle retries or error logging.

Code Example (GenServer for Task Management and Failure Handling):

Elixir

```elixir
defmodule Emailer do

  use GenServer

  def init(state) do

    {:ok, state}

  end

      def handle_cast({:send_email, email_address, message}, state) do

    Task.start_linked(fn -> Email.deliver(email_address, message) end)

    {:noreply, state}

  end

  def handle_info({:EXIT, task, reason}, state) do

    IO.inspect("Email delivery failed: #{reason}")
```

```elixir
    # Log the error or potentially retry sending the email
(implement logic here)

    {:noreply, state}

  end

end
```

In this example, the **Emailer** GenServer receives requests to send emails. It starts linked tasks for each request and handles failure notifications (:EXIT messages) by logging the error. You can extend this by implementing logic for retrying failed emails.

2. **Using Timeouts with Canceled Tasks:**
- **Graceful Cancellation:** While timeouts are essential, abruptly stopping a task can lead to inconsistencies. Utilize Task.cancel/1 to gracefully terminate a timed-out task, allowing it to potentially clean up resources before exiting.

Code Example (Task with Timeout and Cancellation):

Elixir

```elixir
def generate_report_with_timeout(data) do

        {:ok,     task}    =     Task.start(fn     ->
generate_complex_report(data) end, timeout: 10000)

  receive do

    {:ok, report} ->
```

```
# Process the report

after

10000 ->

  Task.cancel(task)

    IO.puts("Report generation timed out. Cleaning up
resources...")

    # Implement logic to clean up any resources used by
the task (e.g., database connections)

  end

end
```

In this example, the task generates a report. If successful, the report is processed. If the task times out, it's canceled, and a message is printed. You can further enhance this by adding code to clean up resources used by the task before it exits.

3. **Error Handling in Tasks with try...rescue:**
- **Catching Errors within Tasks:** Tasks themselves can benefit from error handling using **try...rescue** blocks. This allows you to catch specific exceptions and potentially handle them gracefully, preventing the entire task from failing.

Code Example (Task with Error Handling using try...rescue):

Elixir

```elixir
def update_user_profile(user_id, updates) do

  Task.start(fn ->

    try

      User.update(user_id, updates)

    rescue

      # Handle specific exceptions (e.g., database connection errors)

        # Log the error or potentially retry the update (implement logic here)

    end

  end)

end
```

In this example, the task updates a user profile. The try...rescue block allows you to catch potential exceptions and implement appropriate handling (logging or retry logic).

Note:

- Asynchronous tasks are powerful, but failures can happen.

- Link and monitor tasks or use GenServers for structured task management.
- Use timeouts with graceful cancellation to prevent indefinitely running tasks.
- Write robust task code with try...rescue to catch and handle errors gracefully.

By employing these techniques, you can build fault-tolerant Elixir applications that are responsive and handle task failures effectively, ensuring a smooth user experience even when background jobs encounter issues.

6.3 Advanced Tasking Techniques for Complex Backend Operations:

In Elixir, asynchronous tasks have become a cornerstone for building scalable and responsive backend applications. But as your applications grow, so do the complexities of managing background operations. This section dives into advanced tasking techniques to tackle even the most challenging backend workflows.

1. Leveraging GenServers for Task Management:

- **GenServers as Task Orchestrators:** While the Task module provides the foundation for tasks, GenServers offer a more structured approach for managing them. A GenServer can act as a task supervisor, managing a pool of worker processes, handling task scheduling, and coordinating communication between tasks.
- **Benefits of GenServers:**

- Task Queues and Prioritization: GenServers allow you to implement task queues, enabling you to prioritize tasks and ensure critical operations are executed first.
- Error Handling and Retries: GenServers can be configured to handle task failures gracefully, potentially retrying failed tasks or logging errors for further investigation.

Code Example (GenServer with Task Queue and Retry Logic):

Elixir

```elixir
defmodule ImageProcessor do

  use GenServer

  def init(state) do

    {:ok, state, {:queue, []}}  # Initialize with an empty queue

  end

  def handle_cast({:process_image, image_path}, state) do

    {:noreply, update_state(state, {:queue, [image_path | state.queue]})}

  end

  def handle_info({:task_failed, image_path, reason}, state) do
```

```
IO.inspect("Image processing failed for #{image_path}:
#{reason}")

  # Implement logic to potentially retry the task (e.g., after
a delay)

  {:noreply, state}

end

  # ... (Functions to process tasks from the queue and
handle retries)

end
```

In this example, the **ImageProcessor** GenServer manages a queue of image paths for processing. Tasks are added to the queue, and the GenServer handles processing them one by one. The **handle_info** function implements logic for handling task failures, potentially retrying them.

2. Building Asynchronous Pipelines with GenStage:

- **Composing Tasks with GenStage:** GenStage is a powerful framework for building asynchronous pipelines. It allows you to chain tasks together, where the output of one task becomes the input for the next.
- **Benefits of GenStage:**
  - **Modular and Reusable Stages:** Tasks can be encapsulated as GenStage stages, promoting modularity and reusability in your code.
  - **Error Handling and Supervision:** GenStage provides built-in error handling mechanisms, ensuring the pipeline gracefully recovers from failures in individual stages.

Code Example (Simple GenStage Pipeline for Data Processing):

Elixir

```
defmodule DataPipeline do

  use GenStage

  def init(state) do

    {:ok, state}

  end

  def handle_call({:process_data, data}, _from, state) do

    {:noreply, {:forward, data}, state}

  end

  # ... (Define stages for data cleaning, transformation, and storage)

end
```

In this example, the **DataPipeline** GenStage defines stages for processing data. The **handle_call** function initiates the pipeline by forwarding the data to the first stage. Each subsequent stage can process the output from the previous stage, forming an asynchronous pipeline.

3. Utilizing Supervision Strategies for Task Management:

- **The Task.Supervisor Revisited:** The Task.Supervisor plays a crucial role in advanced tasking. You can define supervision strategies that dictate how the supervisor handles failures within tasks or worker processes it manages.

- **Supervision Strategies:**
  - :one_for_one: Restarts only the failing task, allowing others to continue.
  - :one_for_all: Restarts all managed processes if one fails (useful for tightly coupled tasks).
  - **Custom Strategies:** You can define custom strategies for more granular control over restarts.

Note:

- Advanced tasking techniques empower you to manage complex backend operations.
- Leverage GenServers for structured task management, prioritization, and error handling.
- Utilize GenStage for building asynchronous pipelines with modular and reusable stages.
- Employ the Task.Supervisor with appropriate supervision strategies for robust task execution.

More Examples and Codes for practical purposes

1. GenServer with Rate Limiting:

This example showcases a GenServer that processes tasks while implementing rate limiting to avoid overloading a service.

Elixir

```elixir
defmodule Throttler do

  use GenServer

  def init(state) do

      {:ok, state, max_requests: 10, rate_limit_window: 1000}

  end


  def handle_cast({:process_request}, state) do

    current_time = System.monotonic_time()

    if allowed?(state, current_time) do

      {:noreply, update_state(state, requests: state.requests + 1, timestamp: current_time)}

    else

      {:noreply, state}  # Reject request if rate limit is reached

    end

  end

  # Function to check if processing is allowed based on rate limit window and request count

  defp allowed?(state, current_time) do

    requests = state.requests
```

```elixir
        window_start = current_time -
state.rate_limit_window

        requests_in_window = state.requests -
Enum.count(state.requests, &(&1 > window_start))

  requests_in_window < state.max_requests

 end

end
```

2. GenStage with Parallel Processing:

This example demonstrates a GenStage pipeline that processes data in parallel using multiple stages.

Elixir

```elixir
defmodule ParallelProcessing do

 use GenStage

 def init(state) do

  {:ok, state, num_workers: 4}

 end

 def handle_call({:process_data, data}, _from, state) do

        {:noreply, {:forward, Enum.split(data,
state.num_workers)}, state}

 end
```

```
# ... (Define stages that process data chunks in parallel
using multiple worker processes)

end
```

3. Task.Supervisor with Restart Strategy:

This example showcases a Task.Supervisor with a custom supervision strategy that restarts only tasks failing more than twice consecutively.

Elixir

```
defmodule ErrorHandlingSupervisor do

  use Task.Supervisor

  def init(_) do

    children = [

      worker(fn -> complex_task(1) end, strategy: :custom)

    ]

      {:ok, children, strategy: {:custom, fn(task, reason,
  _data) ->

      count = Map.get(ReasonTracker, task.pid, 0)

      if count < 2 do

        {:restart, 1000}  # Restart task with a delay

      else
```

```
        {:terminate, reason}  # Terminate task after
exceeding retry limit

    end

  end

  ]}

  end

end
```

These examples provide a glimpse into the power of advanced tasking techniques in Elixir. Remember to adapt and extend these concepts to fit your specific application requirements.

By mastering these advanced tasking techniques, you can create well-structured, scalable, and fault-tolerant Elixir applications that efficiently handle even the most intricate background operations.

Chapter 7: Designing Scalable and Concurrent Systems

We've explored the magic of tasks and channels for handling asynchronous work. Now, buckle up as we delve into the exciting world of building truly scalable and concurrent Elixir applications. Imagine your application is a restaurant – it can handle a few customers at first, but to truly thrive, it needs to expand and serve a growing crowd. That's the essence of scalability!

7.1 Architectural Patterns for Scalable Backend Applications with Elixir

As your Elixir application matures and attracts more users, its ability to handle increased workloads becomes paramount. This section explores architectural patterns that empower you to design and build scalable backend applications in Elixir.

Understanding Scalability:

- **Scalability:** Imagine a small bakery. It can handle a few customers, but on busy weekends, long lines and wait times become inevitable. A scalable bakery can adapt by adding more staff or expanding its kitchen – this is what we strive for in our applications.
- **Two Main Scaling Approaches:**
  - **Vertical Scaling (Scaling Up):** Adding more resources to a single machine (e.g., more CPU cores or memory) can improve performance up

to a limit. It's often less flexible and cost-effective in the long run.

- ○ **Horizontal Scaling (Scaling Out):** Distributing your application across multiple machines (think adding more bakery locations) allows you to handle significantly higher loads and improve overall availability.

Architectural Patterns for Scalability:

Elixir offers various architectural patterns to achieve horizontal scalability, each with its strengths:

1. **Supervisory Trees:**
   - ○ **Concept:** Supervisory trees mimic a hierarchical management structure. A supervisor process oversees child processes, ensuring their proper functioning and restarting them if they fail.
   - ○ **Benefits:**
     - ■ **Structured Process Management:** Supervisors provide a clear organization for your application's processes, promoting maintainability and fault tolerance.
     - ■ **Isolation and Restarting:** Supervisors isolate processes, preventing failures in one process from affecting others. Additionally, supervisors can automatically restart failed processes.

Code Example (Simple Supervisory Tree):

Elixir

```elixir
defmodule MyApp do

  use Application

  def start(_type, _args) do

    children = [

      {MyWorker, []},

      {MySupervisor, []}  # Supervisor overseeing the worker

    ]

    {:ok, children}

  end

end


defmodule MySupervisor do

  use Supervisor


  def init(_) do

      {:ok, [worker: {MyWorker, []}]}  # Supervisor with a
child worker process

  end

end
```

2. **GenServer Pools:**
   - **Concept:** Imagine a pool of waiters at a restaurant efficiently handling customer requests. GenServer pools function similarly. A pool consists of multiple worker GenServer processes, sharing a mailbox. Incoming messages are distributed among the available workers, improving concurrency and handling high message volumes.
   - **Benefits:**
     - **Load Balancing and Scalability:** GenServer pools automatically distribute messages, ensuring work is evenly spread across worker processes. You can easily scale a pool by adding more worker GenServers.
     - **Flexibility:** GenServer pools can handle various tasks and provide a structured approach for managing worker processes.

Code Example (Simple GenServer Pool):

Elixir

```elixir
defmodule EmailerPool do

  use GenServer

  def init(state) do

    {:ok, state, {:pool, size: 4}}  # Create a pool with 4 worker GenServers
```

```
end

    def    handle_cast({:send_email,    email_address,
message}, state) do

        {:noreply,  GenServer.cast(pool_worker_pid(state),
{:send_email, email_address, message})}

end

# Function to create and manage worker GenServer
processes within the pool

defp pool_worker_pid(state) do

Enum.find(state.pool, &GenServer.whereis(&1))[:pid]

end

end
```

3. **The Pub/Sub Pattern:**
    - **Concept:** Imagine a central bulletin board in a restaurant kitchen where chefs can post orders. The Pub/Sub (Publish/Subscribe) pattern uses message queues for asynchronous communication between processes. Processes "publish" messages to a topic, and other processes can "subscribe" to that topic to receive messages.
    - **Benefits:**
        - **Loose Coupling:** Processes are loosely coupled, as publishers don't need to

know who subscribes to their messages, promoting modularity and scalability.

- **Asynchronous Communication:** Processes can communicate asynchronously, improving responsiveness and handling high message volumes.

Code Example (Simple Pub/Sub with GenStage):

Elixir

```elixir
defmodule OrderProcessing do

  use GenStage

  def init(_) do

    {:ok, []}

  end

    def handle_call({:place_order, order_data}, _from, state) do

    {:noreply, {:forward, order_data}, state}

  end

end

# Subscribe other GenStages to the "orders" topic to process incoming orders
```

Choosing the Right Pattern:

The best architectural pattern for your application depends on your specific needs. Here's a breakdown to help you choose:

Factors to Consider:

- **Nature of Tasks:** Are your tasks independent (e.g., sending emails) or require coordination (e.g., processing a complex order)?
- **Message Volume:** How many messages will your application handle per second or minute?
- **Fault Tolerance:** How critical is it for your application to recover from process failures?

Pattern Matching:

1. **Supervisory Trees:** Ideal for managing a hierarchical structure of processes with well-defined relationships and restart strategies. Suitable for applications with independent tasks and moderate message volumes.
2. **GenServer Pools:** Effective for handling high volumes of independent messages and scaling efficiently. Well-suited for applications with tasks like processing incoming requests or sending notifications.
3. **The Pub/Sub Pattern:** Excellent for loosely coupled communication between processes and handling asynchronous workflows. Well-aligned with applications requiring distributed processing or real-time updates.

Note:

- You can combine these patterns for a more robust architecture.
- Consider trade-offs between complexity, scalability, and fault tolerance.
- Start with a simple design and evolve as your application grows.

Additional Considerations:

- **OTP Behaviours:** Explore behaviours like GenEvent for structured event handling or GenServer for managing state and handling requests within processes.
- **Distributed OTP:** As your application demands more scalability, delve into distributed OTP features for managing processes across multiple machines.

By understanding these architectural patterns and their strengths, you can make informed decisions when designing your scalable backend applications in Elixir. Remember, the chosen pattern should lay the foundation for an application that can grow and adapt to your ever-increasing user base.

7.2 Horizontal Scaling and Distributing Processes Across Machines:

Imagine your Elixir application is a bustling restaurant. It started small, but now the lines are out the door! Vertical scaling, adding more power to a single server (like a bigger kitchen), can only take you so far. This section explores horizontal scaling, the secret ingredient for handling massive user growth in Elixir applications.

Understanding Horizontal Scaling:

- **The Limits of Vertical Scaling:** Throwing more hardware (CPU, memory) at a single server can improve performance, but it has limitations. Costs increase, and eventually, you hit a physical bottleneck.
- **Horizontal Scaling to the Rescue:** Imagine opening new restaurants (adding more servers) to handle the customer influx. Horizontal scaling distributes your application workload across multiple machines, significantly increasing capacity and improving overall availability.

Key Concepts for Horizontal Scaling:

1. **OTP Releases:**
   - **Concept:** An OTP release packages your entire application code, configurations, and dependencies into a deployable unit. Think of it as a blueprint for replicating your restaurant across different locations.
   - **Benefits:**
     - **Standardized Deployment:** OTP releases ensure consistent application behavior across all deployed machines, simplifying deployments and updates.

- **Isolation and Fault Tolerance:** Processes on one machine are isolated from others. If a single machine fails, others can continue serving requests, minimizing downtime.

Code Example (Simple OTP Release Structure):

```
my_app/
  ├── apps/
  │    └── my_app/
  │        ├── lib/
  │        │    └── my_app.ex
  │        └── mix.exs
  └── rel/
       └── my_app/
           ├── OTP.app
           └── start.erl
```

2. **Distributed Erlang (OTP):**
   - **Concept:** Distributed Erlang (OTP) extends the capabilities of Erlang (the language underlying Elixir) to manage processes across multiple

machines. It provides features for communication, supervision, and failure handling in a distributed environment.

- ○ **Benefits:**
  - ■ **Scalability and Fault Tolerance:** OTP allows you to seamlessly scale your application by adding more machines. It also provides mechanisms for handling process failures and ensuring application availability.

Exploring Distributed OTP is a more advanced topic, but here are some key features:

- :inet **application:** Enables communication between processes on different machines using network protocols.
- :cookie **application:** Provides a mechanism for distributed processes to identify each other securely.
- :supervisor **application:** Extends supervision capabilities to manage processes across multiple machines.

Horizontal scaling requires additional planning and infrastructure considerations compared to vertical scaling.

Benefits of Horizontal Scaling:

- **Increased Capacity:** Handle significantly higher workloads by distributing the application across multiple machines.

- **Improved Availability:** If one machine fails, others can continue serving requests, minimizing downtime for your users.
- **Elasticity:** Scale your application up or down based on your needs. Easily add or remove servers as your user base grows or shrinks.

Code Examples for Horizontal Scaling

1. Simple OTP Release Structure (Expanded):

```
my_app/
  ├── apps/
  |    └── my_app/
  |        ├── lib/
  |        |   ├── my_app_worker.ex  # Worker process code
  |        |   └── my_app_supervisor.ex # Supervisor process code
  |        └── mix.exs # Application build configuration
  └── rel/
      └── my_app/
          ├── OTP.app  # Application configuration file
          └── start.erl # Startup script for the release
```

This example shows a more detailed release structure with separate files for worker processes, supervisors, and application configuration.

2. Sample Code for Distributed Communication with :inet (Basic Example):

Elixir

```elixir
defmodule MyAppWorker do

  def start(server_address) do

      {:ok, pid} = spawn_link(__MODULE__, :work, [server_address])

    Process.register(pid, :my_app_worker)

  end

  def work(server_address) do

   # ... perform some work

    {:ok, response} = :gen_tcp.send(server_address, "Hello from worker!")

    IO.inspect(response)

  end

end
```

This code showcases a simple worker process that can connect and send a message to a server process running on a different machine using the :inet application.

Note: A complete example for distributed communication would involve a server process listening for incoming connections and responding to messages. This is a simplified illustration of the concept.

These examples provide a glimpse into horizontal scaling with Elixir. A thorough understanding of OTP releases and Distributed OTP is crucial for real-world implementations.

By embracing horizontal scaling and leveraging tools like OTP releases and Distributed Erlang, you can build Elixir applications that can truly scale to meet the demands of even the most successful ventures. Remember, a well-architected and horizontally scalable application can ensure your creation thrives as your user base flourishes!

7.3 Optimizing Resource Utilization for High Performance:

Scaling your Elixir application horizontally with multiple machines is fantastic, but it's not the only path to high performance. Just like a well-oiled machine in your kitchen, optimizing resource utilization within your application can significantly boost its efficiency. This section explores techniques to ensure your Elixir code runs smoothly and delivers exceptional performance.

Understanding Resource Utilization:

- **Resource Utilization:** Imagine the efficiency of your kitchen staff. Are they constantly busy, or are there periods of idleness? Resource utilization refers to how effectively your application uses the available processing power, memory, and other resources.
- **The Importance of Optimization:** Even with horizontal scaling, inefficient code can lead to wasted resources and bottlenecks. By optimizing your application, you can handle more work with the same resources or achieve faster response times.

Techniques for Optimization:

1. **Monitoring and Profiling:**
   - **Concept:** Just like monitoring your kitchen staff's workflow, application monitoring tools like Exometer and cprof help you identify performance bottlenecks.
   - **Benefits:**
     - **Identifying Performance Issues:** Monitoring tools can pinpoint areas where your application spends excessive time or memory, allowing you to focus optimization efforts.
     - **Understanding Resource Usage:** These tools provide insights into how your application utilizes CPU, memory, and other resources.

Code Example (Using Exometer):

```
# Install Exometer

mix dote install exometer

# Start your application with monitoring

iex MyApp -e Exometer.start
```

2. **Code Optimization:**
   - **Concept:** Review and improve your code to ensure it's efficient and utilizes resources effectively.
   - **Optimization Techniques:**
     - **Avoiding Unnecessary Function Calls:** Minimize redundant function calls, as each function call incurs some overhead.
     - **Choosing Efficient Data Structures:** Select data structures (like maps or lists) that are well-suited for your specific use case and operations.
     - **Algorithms and Complexity:** Consider the time and space complexity of algorithms you use. Choose algorithms with lower complexities for frequently executed tasks.

Code Example (Simple Optimization):

Elixir

```
# Less efficient (iterates over the list multiple times)

def sum_squares(list) do
```

```
  list |> Enum.map(&(&1 * &1)) |> Enum.sum

end

# More efficient (uses reduce to iterate once)

def sum_squares(list) do

  Enum.reduce(list, 0, &(&1 + (&2 * &2)))

end
```

3. **Leveraging Elixir Features:**
   - **Concept:** Elixir offers built-in features that promote efficient concurrency and resource utilization.
   - **Techniques:**
     - **GenStage for Pipelines:** Break down complex tasks into smaller stages using **GenStage**. This allows for efficient parallel processing and avoids blocking operations.
     - **Task.Supervisor for Task Management:** Utilize the **Task.Supervisor** to manage tasks with appropriate supervision strategies. This helps prevent resource exhaustion by limiting the number of concurrent tasks.

Additional Code Examples for Resource Utilization Optimization

1. Profiling with cprof:

```
# Run your application with profiling enabled

iex MyApp --profile

# Analyze the generated `.prof` file to identify performance bottlenecks

cprof my_app.prof
```

2. Efficient Data Structure Usage:

Elixir

```
# Using a map for fast lookups by key

user_data = %{id: 1, name: "John Doe"}

# Using a list for ordered data (less efficient for lookups)

ordered_tasks = ["task1", "task2", "task3"]
```

3. GenStage Pipeline Example:

Elixir

```
defmodule DataProcessingPipeline do

  use GenStage

  def init(_) do

    {:ok, []}

  end
```

```elixir
def handle_call({:process_data, data}, _from, state) do

  {:noreply, {:forward, data}, state}

 end

end

# Define additional stages for data transformation and
filtering

# ...

# Connect stages to form a processing pipeline

data_processing_pipeline =

 DataProcessingPipeline |>

 GenStage.into(AnotherStage) |>

 GenStage.into(FinalStage)
```

4. Task.Supervisor with Restart Strategy:

Elixir

```elixir
defmodule LongRunningTaskSupervisor do

 use Task.Supervisor

 def init(_) do

    {:ok, [worker: {LongRunningTask, []}, strategy:
:one_for_one]}
```

```
  end

end

# The `:one_for_one` strategy restarts only the failing
task
```

These are just a few examples to illustrate the concepts. Remember, the specific optimization techniques will vary depending on your application's needs and the identified bottlenecks.

Optimization is an ongoing process. As your application evolves, revisit these techniques and adapt them to your specific needs.

By employing a combination of monitoring, code optimization, and leveraging Elixir's built-in features, you can ensure your Elixir application runs at peak performance, delivering a smooth and efficient user experience even under heavy loads.

Chapter 8: Concurrency for Common Backend Operations

In today's fast-paced world, users expect responsive and efficient backend applications. This chapter explores how to leverage concurrency patterns in Elixir to handle common backend operations concurrently, significantly improving your application's performance and scalability.

Understanding Concurrency:

- **Concurrency:** Imagine a skilled chef multitasking in the kitchen – chopping vegetables while a pot simmers on the stove. Concurrency refers to the ability of a program to handle multiple tasks seemingly simultaneously. In Elixir, this allows your application to process multiple requests or operations without blocking each other.

8.1 Handling API Requests Concurrently:

Imagine your Elixir application is a bustling restaurant. Customers (API requests) keep pouring in, but your waiters (traditional request handling) can only serve them one at a time. This leads to long waits and frustrated customers (users). Concurrency in Elixir comes to the rescue, allowing your application to handle multiple API requests simultaneously, just like a well-oiled restaurant kitchen.

The Sequential Struggle:

- **Traditional Approach:** In a traditional approach, each incoming API request might follow these steps:
    1. The request arrives.
    2. The main thread of your application processes the request (e.g., fetches data, performs calculations).
    3. The application sends the response back to the user.
    4. The main thread waits for the next request before moving on.

This sequential approach can be slow, especially under heavy load. Each request has to wait for the previous one to finish before it can be processed. It's like having only one waiter handling all the customers in a busy restaurant.

The Power of Concurrency:

- **Concurrent Request Handling:** Concurrency allows your application to handle multiple requests seemingly at the same time. Here's how it works:
    1. The request arrives.
    2. Instead of blocking the main thread, the application spawns a separate process (like an additional waiter) to handle the request.
    3. The main thread becomes free to handle the next incoming request.
    4. The spawned process finishes handling the original request and sends the response back to the user.

This approach significantly improves performance. While one request is being processed, the main thread can handle others, just like a restaurant with multiple waiters can serve multiple customers simultaneously.

GenServer Pools: The Waiter Brigade for Your API:

- **GenServer:** A GenServer is a powerful actor in Elixir that excels at handling concurrent requests. It's like having a dedicated manager (the GenServer) overseeing a pool of worker processes (the waiters).
- **GenServer Pool:** A GenServer pool is a collection of worker GenServer processes managed by a single supervisor GenServer. This allows you to easily scale your API handling by adding more worker processes to the pool. It's like having a team of waiters managed by a head waiter who can adjust the team size based on customer influx.

Benefits of Concurrency with GenServer Pools:

- **Improved Responsiveness:** Users experience faster response times as your application can handle multiple requests without waiting for each one to finish entirely.
- **Increased Scalability:** As your user base grows, you can easily add more worker processes to the GenServer pool to handle the increased load.
- **Isolation and Fault Tolerance:** Each worker process operates in isolation, preventing failures in one request from affecting others. Additionally, GenServers can be configured to restart automatically upon failure, ensuring high availability for your API endpoints.

Code Example (Simple GenServer Pool for API Requests):

Elixir

```elixir
defmodule ApiRequestHandler do

  use GenServer

  def init(_) do

    {:ok, []}

  end

    def handle_call({:handle_request, request}, _from, state) do

      # Process the API request (replace with actual request handling logic)

    response = process_request(request)

    {:noreply, response, state}

  end

end

# Create a GenServer pool with multiple worker processes

GenServer.start_link({ApiRequestHandler, []}, name: :api_request_handler_pool)
```

```elixir
# In your Phoenix controller, handle incoming requests by
sending them to the GenServer pool

def handle_request(conn, %{"data" => data}) do

        GenServer.cast(:api_request_handler_pool,
{:handle_request, data})

  # Respond to the user with an acknowledgement message
while the request is processed concurrently

  conn |> json(%{message: "Request processing..."})

end
```

Additional Code Examples for Concurrent API Request Handling

1. GenServer Pool with Supervision Strategy:

Elixir

```elixir
defmodule ApiRequestHandlerSupervisor do

  use Supervisor

  def init(_) do

    worker = {ApiRequestHandler, []}
```

```elixir
  supervisor_strategy = :one_for_one

  {:ok, [{worker: worker, strategy: supervisor_strategy}]}

 end

end
```

This supervisor strategy restarts only the failing worker process

```elixir
GenServer.start_link({ApiRequestHandlerSupervisor, []})
```

2. Handling Large Requests with Timeouts:

Elixir

```elixir
defmodule ApiRequestHandler do

 use GenServer

  def handle_call({:handle_request, request}, _from, state) do

   {:noreply, {:reply, process_request(request)}, state} |>
timeout(5000)

 end

 def handle_info({:timeout, _}, state) do

  {:noreply, {:reply, {:error, "Request timed out"}}, state}

 end

end
```

This example sets a timeout of 5 seconds for request processing

3. Sending Responses Asynchronously:

Elixir

```elixir
defmodule ApiRequestHandler do

  use GenServer

    def handle_call({:handle_request, request}, _from, state) do

        Task.start(fn -> process_request(request) |> send_response(conn) end)

    {:noreply, :ok, state}

  end


  defp send_response(response) do

    # Send the response back to the user (replace with actual logic)

  end
end
```

This approach avoids blocking the GenServer process while sending the response

These are simplified examples. Real-world implementations will involve additional logic for handling specific request types and error scenarios.

Concurrency is a powerful tool, but it's crucial to design your concurrent request handling with care. Consider factors like potential race conditions (when multiple processes try to access the same data at the same time) and implement appropriate synchronization mechanisms if needed.

8.2 Concurrent Database Interactions with Elixir:

In today's data-driven world, efficient interaction with your database is crucial for a performant Elixir application. But waiting for each database operation to complete sequentially can slow things down. This section explores concurrent database interactions with Elixir, allowing you to fetch and store data without sacrificing speed.

The Sequential Struggle:

- **Traditional Approach:** Imagine your application needs to fetch data for multiple users. In a traditional approach, you might loop through each user ID, one by one, performing a separate database query for each.

This sequential approach can be inefficient, especially for large datasets or high traffic. Each query has to wait for the previous one to finish before it can be executed, leading to bottlenecks and slow response times.

The Power of Concurrency for Database Interactions:

- **Concurrent Database Access:** Concurrency allows your application to perform multiple database operations seemingly at the same time. Here's how it works:
    1. Your application prepares multiple database queries (e.g., to fetch data for different users).
    2. Instead of executing them one by one, it utilizes techniques like asynchronous processing to send these queries to the database concurrently.
    3. While the database processes the queries, your application can focus on other tasks.
    4. As the database finishes each query, it sends the results back to your application.

This approach significantly improves performance. Your application isn't blocked waiting for each query to complete, allowing it to handle other tasks concurrently.

Ecto and Asynchronous Database Interactions:

- **Ecto:** Ecto is a popular Elixir library that simplifies database interactions. It also provides features for handling database operations asynchronously.
- async: true **Option:** Ecto functions like Ecto.Repo.insert_all/2 (for inserting data) or Ecto.Repo.update_all/2 (for updating data) can be

used with the async: true option. This instructs Ecto to perform the operation asynchronously, freeing up your application thread.

Benefits of Concurrent Database Interactions:

- **Improved Performance:** By utilizing concurrency, you can significantly reduce the time it takes to fetch or store data, leading to faster response times for your users.
- **Increased Scalability:** As your application grows and handles more data, concurrent database interactions can help maintain performance without requiring constant database upgrades.
- **Efficient Resource Utilization:** While waiting for database responses, your application can focus on other tasks, making better use of available resources.

Code Example (Concurrent Inserts with Ecto):

Elixir

data_to_insert = # List of data to insert

Ecto.Repo.insert_all(data_to_insert, async: true)

Your application can continue processing other tasks while the inserts happen concurrently

process_other_tasks()

Additional Code Examples for Concurrent Database Interactions

1. Handling Large Datasets with Batching:

Elixir

```
defmodule UserRepository do

 def fetch_users_by_ids(ids) do

  chunked_ids = Enum.chunk(ids, 100)  # Chunk IDs into batches of 100

  tasks = Enum.map(chunked_ids, fn(id_batch) ->

   Task.async(fn -> Ecto.Repo.all(User, id: id_batch) end)

  end)

  Enum.map(tasks, &Task.await/1) |> List.flatten

 end

end


# This example retrieves users in batches to avoid overwhelming the database
```

2. Combining Concurrency with Transactions:

Elixir

```elixir
defmodule OrderRepository do
  def create_order_with_items(order_data, items) do
    Ecto.Multi.new
    |> Ecto.Multi.insert(:order, order_data)
    |> Ecto.Multi.insert_all(:items, items, async: true)
    |> Ecto.Repo.transaction
  end
end

# This example uses a transaction with concurrent inserts
for efficiency
```

3. Error Handling and Retries for Asynchronous Operations:

Elixir

```elixir
defmodule UserRepository do
  def create_user(user_data) do
    Ecto.Repo.insert(user_data, async: true) |> handle_insert_result
  end
```

```
defp handle_insert_result({:ok, _user}) do

  {:ok, "User created successfully"}

end

defp handle_insert_result({:error, reason, _}) do

      # Implement retry logic or handle the error
appropriately

  {:error, reason}

end

end

# This example demonstrates basic error handling for
asynchronous inserts
```

These are just a few examples to illustrate concurrent database interactions. For complex scenarios, consider using libraries like Oban for distributed task management and robust retry strategies.

Concurrency can be a double-edged sword. Consider factors like potential race conditions (when multiple processes try to modify the same data at the same time) and implement appropriate data access patterns to ensure data integrity.

By adopting concurrent database interactions with Ecto, you can create responsive and efficient Elixir applications that handle database operations smoothly, even with large datasets or high traffic.

8.3 Processing Background Jobs with Efficient Concurrency Patterns:

In modern web applications, background jobs play a crucial role in handling asynchronous tasks like sending emails, processing uploads, or generating reports. These tasks are essential but should not impede the responsiveness of the main application thread. This section explores efficient concurrency patterns in Elixir for handling background jobs, ensuring smooth operation and optimal resource utilization.

Understanding Sequential Processing Limitations:

- **Sequential Approach:** A traditional approach might involve processing background jobs sequentially. Each job waits for the previous one to finish before it can begin execution.

Consider this analogy: Imagine a busy restaurant with a single dishwasher. Each dirty dish (background job) has to wait its turn to be cleaned (processed) before the next one can be added to the queue. This sequential processing can lead to bottlenecks, especially under heavy load, as jobs pile up waiting for their turn.

The Power of Concurrency:

- **Concurrent Processing:** Concurrency allows your application to distribute background jobs across multiple worker processes for parallel execution. These worker processes operate independently, handling jobs simultaneously, significantly improving overall processing speed.

Think of it this way: The same restaurant now has multiple dishwashers working concurrently. Dirty dishes (background jobs) can be cleaned (processed) in parallel, significantly reducing the waiting time for each dish (job).

Leveraging Elixir's Concurrency Tools:

Elixir provides powerful tools to implement efficient concurrent processing for background jobs:

1. **GenStage Pipelines:** GenStage is a framework for building composable processing stages. Complex background jobs can be broken down into smaller, independent stages that can be executed concurrently. This modular approach allows for efficient parallel processing and easier handling of failures within individual stages.
2. **Task Supervisor:** The Task Supervisor is a robust mechanism for managing background tasks as supervised processes. It provides features for automatic process restarts in case of failures, ensuring job completion even if individual worker

processes encounter errors. Additionally, the Task Supervisor allows for dynamic scaling by adjusting the number of worker processes based on workload demands.

Benefits of Concurrent Background Job Processing:

- **Improved Performance:** Concurrent processing significantly reduces overall processing time for background jobs, leading to a more responsive application for users.
- **Increased Scalability:** As your application workload grows, you can easily scale by adding more worker processes to handle the increased job volume.
- **Enhanced Fault Tolerance:** The Task Supervisor ensures job completion even if individual worker processes fail, promoting application robustness.

Example: Concurrent Email Sending with GenStage **and** Task **Supervisor:**

Elixir

```
defmodule Emailer do

  use GenStage

  def init(_) do

    {:ok, []}

  end
```

```elixir
  def handle_call({:send_email, email_data}, _from,
state) do

   {:noreply, email_data, state}

  end

end

# Define additional stages for email validation,
templating, and sending

# ...

# Connect stages to form a processing pipeline for emails

email_processing_pipeline =

  Emailer |>

  GenStage.into(ValidationStage) |>

  GenStage.into(TemplatingStage) |>

  GenStage.into(SendingStage)

# Start the `Task` Supervisor with worker processes for the
pipeline

Task.Supervisor.start_link(name:
:email_sender_supervisor)

def send_email(email_data) do

              GenServer.cast(:email_sender_supervisor,
{:send_email, email_data})
```

end

Additional Examples and Code for Concurrent Background Jobs

1. Dynamic Scaling with Task.Supervisor:

Elixir

```elixir
defmodule LongRunningTaskSupervisor do

  use Task.Supervisor

  def init(_) do

    # Define a function to determine the number of worker
    processes based on workload

    worker_count = get_worker_count()

    workers = Enum.map(1..worker_count, fn(_) ->
    {LongRunningTask, []} end)

    strategy = :one_for_one

    {:ok, workers, strategy}

  end
end

# This example dynamically adjusts the number of worker
processes based on workload
```

2. Handling Job Failures with Retries:

Elixir

```elixir
defmodule ImageProcessingJob do

  def process_image(image_data) do

    # Implement image processing logic

    # ...

  rescue

    exception -> handle_exception(exception, image_data)

  end

  defp handle_exception(exception, image_data) do

    # Implement retry logic or error handling for failed jobs

    IO.puts("Error processing image: #{exception.message}")

    # Consider retrying the job with exponential backoff

  end

end
```

This example demonstrates basic error handling and potential retry logic for failed jobs

3. Sending Notifications with Broadcasting:

Elixir

```elixir
defmodule NotificationService do

  use GenServer

  def init(_) do

    {:ok, []}

  end

  def handle_call({:send_notification, message}, _from,
state) do

    broadcast(:notifications, message)

    {:noreply, :ok, state}

  end

end


# Define a process for subscribing to notification
broadcasts

defmodule NotificationSubscriber do

  use GenServer

  def init(_) do

    {:ok, subscribe(:notifications)}

  end
```

```elixir
def handle_info({:notification, message}, state) do

    # Handle received notification (e.g., send push
notification to user)

  {:noreply, state}

 end

end
```

This example utilizes broadcasting for real-time notification delivery

These are just a few examples to illustrate different approaches for concurrent background job processing. The specific implementation will depend on the nature of your background tasks and desired behavior. Consider using libraries like **Oban** for complex distributed task management scenarios.

Concurrency is a powerful tool, but it's crucial to design your background job processing with care. Consider factors like potential race conditions (when multiple processes try to access the same data at the same time) and implement appropriate synchronization mechanisms if needed.

By adopting efficient concurrency patterns with **GenStage** pipelines and the **Task** Supervisor, you can create highly scalable and performant Elixir applications that handle background jobs effectively, ensuring a smooth user experience even with a high volume of asynchronous tasks.

Chapter 9: Conquering the Chaos: Testing and Monitoring Concurrent Applications

Alright, you've built this amazing Elixir application that tackles tasks simultaneously, like a superhero juggling flaming chainsaws (metaphorically, of course). But how do you ensure it all works together smoothly, without things catching fire (literally or figuratively)? That's where testing and monitoring come in!

This chapter will equip you with the tools to become a debugging detective, sniffing out any potential issues in your concurrent system. We'll cover strategies for testing, techniques for monitoring, and even tips for troubleshooting common problems. So, grab your magnifying glass and let's dive in!

9.1 Strategies for Testing Concurrent Applications

Testing concurrent applications can feel like navigating a maze – you need a plan to ensure everything works as expected, especially when multiple processes are running simultaneously. This section explores various testing strategies to catch potential issues and ensure your Elixir application functions smoothly under concurrent workloads.

Understanding the Testing Landscape:

- **Traditional Testing Challenges:** In a traditional, sequential application, testing involves providing inputs and verifying the expected outputs. However, with concurrency, multiple processes can interact and modify data, making it trickier to predict behavior.

Imagine this: Testing a program that adds numbers sequentially is straightforward. You provide numbers (inputs) and verify the sum (output). But testing a program that adds numbers concurrently can be more complex. What if two processes try to add to the same value at the same time?

Core Testing Strategies:

1. **Unit Testing:** The foundation of good testing practices. Unit tests isolate individual functions and processes, allowing you to verify their behavior in a controlled environment, even when running concurrently.
- **Think of it this way:** Before attempting your juggling act with flaming chainsaws, you'd want to ensure each chainsaw functions properly on its own. Unit tests are like testing each chainsaw individually.

Code Example (Simple Unit Test for a Concurrent Function):

Elixir

```
defmodule MyConcurrentFunctionTest do
```

```elixir
use ExUnit.Case

test "handles multiple calls concurrently" do

  assert MyModule.concurrent_function(1) == :ok

  assert MyModule.concurrent_function(2) == :ok

end

end
```

In this example, we test if **MyModule.concurrent_function** handles multiple calls concurrently without errors.

2. **Integration Testing:** Once you're confident in your individual components, it's time to see how they perform together. Integration tests simulate real-world scenarios where multiple processes interact concurrently. This helps identify potential conflicts or unexpected behavior that unit tests might miss.

- **Continuing the juggling analogy:** After testing each chainsaw, you'd want to see how you can juggle them all simultaneously. Integration tests are like practicing your juggling act with all the chainsaws lit, ensuring no collisions occur.

3. **Property-Based Testing:** This powerful technique goes beyond specific test cases. It defines properties that your application should always hold true, regardless of the data it receives. By testing these properties with random data generation, you can uncover hidden edge cases that traditional tests might miss.

- **Imagine this:** Instead of just testing your juggling act with specific weights for the chainsaws, property-based testing would ensure you can handle chainsaws of any weight, within a defined range. This helps uncover potential issues that might arise with unexpected data.

Benefits of Property-Based Testing:

- **Improved Test Coverage:** Tests a wider range of possible inputs and scenarios compared to traditional test cases.
- **Early Detection of Issues:** Can uncover hidden edge cases that might not be apparent with specific test data.
- **Increased Confidence:** Provides greater confidence in the overall robustness of your concurrent application.

Example Property for a Concurrent Counter:

Elixir

```
property "concurrent increments should result in correct total" do

 for _ <- 1..100 do

  counter = Agent.start_link(fn -> 0 end)

  spawn(fn -> Agent.get_and_update(counter, &(&1 + 1))
end)

  spawn(fn -> Agent.get_and_update(counter, &(&1 + 1))
end)
```

```elixir
  assert Agent.get(counter) == 2

 end

end
```

Additional Examples and Code for Testing Concurrent Applications

1. Testing Message Passing with Mocks:

Elixir

```elixir
defmodule MyWorkerTest do

 use ExUnit.Case

 test "processes messages concurrently" do

  mock_receiver = Mock.spy(receive do

   message -> message

  end)

  MyWorker.start_link(mock_receiver)

  send MyWorker, :do_work, "message 1"

  send MyWorker, :do_work, "message 2"

  Mock.verify(mock_receiver, calls: [

   {"message 1"},

   {"message 2"}
```

```
])
```

  end

end

This example uses **Mock** to simulate a message receiver and verifies if the worker process sends messages concurrently.

2. Property-Based Testing with Elixir Property Testing Library:

Elixir

```
defmodule MyConcurrentListTest do

  use ExUnit.Case

  use EProp

  prop "concurrent inserts maintain list order" do

    for _ <- 1..100 do

      values = Enum.random(1..1000)

      list = Agent.start_link(fn -> [] end)

      for value <- values do

          spawn(fn -> Agent.get_and_update(list, &(&1 ++ [value])) end)

      end

      assert Enum.sort(Agent.get(list)) == values
```

```
    end

  end

end
```

This example utilizes the **Elixir Property Testing** library to define a property that ensures concurrent insertions into a list (using an Agent) maintain the correct order of elements.

3. Testing Fault Tolerance with GenServer Exits:

Elixir

```
defmodule MySupervisorTest do

  use ExUnit.Case

  test "restarts worker on process exit" do

    {:ok, _pid} = MyWorker.start_link()

    Process.exit(_pid, :kill)

      assert Supervisor.restart(MySupervisor, :worker) != :ignore

  end

end
```

This example tests if the **MySupervisor** restarts the **MyWorker** process when it exits unexpectedly. This helps ensure fault tolerance in your concurrent application.

These are just a few examples to illustrate testing strategies for concurrent applications. The specific approach will depend on the nature of your application and the types of interactions between processes.

Testing concurrent applications requires a combination of unit testing, integration testing, and potentially property-based testing. By employing these strategies, you can ensure your application behaves as expected, even when multiple processes are juggling tasks simultaneously.

9.2 Monitoring Techniques for Identifying Bottlenecks and Ensuring Application Health

Just like a car dashboard keeps you informed about your engine temperature and fuel level, monitoring tools are crucial for understanding the health of your concurrent Elixir application. They help you identify potential bottlenecks and performance issues before they impact your users. This section explores various monitoring techniques to keep your application running smoothly.

Understanding the Monitoring Landscape:

- **The Importance of Visibility:** In a sequential application, you can often pinpoint performance issues by simply observing its behavior. However, with concurrency, multiple processes interact, making it trickier to identify where things might be slowing down.

Imagine this: Diagnosing a car issue is easier if you can see the engine directly. But in a complex concurrent application, the "engine" is spread across multiple processes. Monitoring provides the tools to see what's happening under the hood.

Core Monitoring Techniques:

1. **Resource Utilization Monitoring:**
   - **CPU Usage:** Tracks how much processing power your application is consuming. High CPU usage can indicate bottlenecks or inefficient code.
   - **Memory Usage:** Monitors how much memory your application is utilizing. Spikes in memory usage might suggest memory leaks or inefficient data structures.
   - **Network Traffic:** Provides insights into incoming and outgoing data transfer. Unusual traffic patterns could signal external service issues or unexpected application behavior.

Monitoring these metrics allows you to identify potential problems and take corrective action, such as optimizing code or scaling resources.

2. **Concurrency Metrics:**
   - **Number of Active Processes:** Tracks the number of processes currently running in your

application. A sudden increase might indicate unexpected behavior or a resource overload.

- ○ **Message Queue Lengths:** Monitors the size of queues used for communication between processes. Long queues can suggest slow processing or bottlenecks in message handling.
- ○ **Process Execution Times:** Provides insights into how long individual processes take to complete tasks. Identifying processes with unusually long execution times can help pinpoint areas for optimization.

By monitoring these concurrency metrics, you can ensure your application's parallel operations are functioning efficiently.

3. **Error Rates:**
   - ○ **Process Crashes:** Tracks the frequency of unexpected process terminations. Frequent crashes might indicate bugs or resource limitations.
   - ○ **API Request Errors:** Monitors the number of failed API requests. An increase in errors could signal issues with external services or your application logic.
   - ○ **Database Errors:** Provides insights into errors encountered during database interactions. These errors might indicate database connection problems or inefficient queries.

Monitoring error rates helps you identify areas for improvement and ensure a reliable user experience.

Monitoring Tools for Elixir:

Several excellent tools can be integrated with Elixir applications for comprehensive monitoring:

- **Prometheus:** A popular open-source toolkit for collecting and analyzing application metrics.
- **Elixir Stats Collector:** A library specifically designed for gathering metrics from Elixir applications.
- **Grafana:** An open-source platform for visualizing and analyzing monitoring data.

Additional Examples and Code for Monitoring Techniques

1. Visualizing Resource Utilization with Grafana:

Imagine you're using Prometheus to collect CPU usage data for your Elixir application. You can then integrate this data with Grafana to create a dashboard visualizing CPU usage over time. This allows you to easily identify spikes or sustained high CPU consumption, potentially indicating bottlenecks.

2. Monitoring Message Queue Lengths with GenServer Monitoring:

Elixir

```
defmodule MyWorkerSupervisor do

  use Supervisor

  def init(_) do
```

```elixir
worker = {MyWorker, [queue_size: :infinity]}

strategy = :one_for_one

    {:ok, [{worker: worker, options: [monitor: :process,
name: :my_worker_monitor]}]}

  end

  def handle_info({:monitor, :process, _, _, _, reason},
state) do

  if reason == :queue_overflow do

    # Handle queue overflow event (e.g., scale up workers)

    {:noreply, state}

  else

    Supervisor.handle_info(reason, state)

  end

  end

end
```

This example utilizes the **monitor: :process** option in the Supervisor child specification to monitor the **MyWorker** process. It defines a custom handle_info callback that specifically checks for the :queue_overflow reason, indicating a full message queue. This allows you to take corrective action when the queue becomes overloaded.

3. Alerting on Error Rates with threshold_notifier:

The **threshold_notifier** library allows you to define thresholds for various metrics and trigger alerts when those thresholds are exceeded. Here's an example for API request errors:

Elixir

```elixir
defmodule ApiErrorAlert do

  use Agent

  def start_link(threshold) do

    Agent.start_link(fn -> 0 end, name: :api_error_count)

    schedule_alert(threshold)

  end

  defp schedule_alert(threshold) do

    Process.send_after(self(), :check_errors, 1000)

  end

  def handle_call(:check_errors, _from) do

    count = Agent.get(:api_error_count)

    if count > threshold do

      # Send alert notification (e.g., email, SMS)

      Agent.put(:api_error_count, 0)
```

```
end

schedule_alert(threshold)

{:noreply, count}

end

end
```

This example utilizes an **Agent** to store the current API error count. It also schedules a check every second (**1000 milliseconds**) to compare the count against a defined threshold. If the threshold is exceeded, an alert notification is triggered.

These are just a few examples to illustrate how you can monitor various aspects of your concurrent application. The specific metrics and tools you choose will depend on your application's needs and complexity.

By leveraging these tools and techniques, you can create a comprehensive monitoring system that keeps you informed about the health and performance of your concurrent Elixir application.

9.3 Debugging and Troubleshooting Common Issues in Concurrent Systems:

Concurrent applications offer incredible power for handling tasks simultaneously, but with great power comes great responsibility (and sometimes, debugging headaches). This section equips you with the knowledge to troubleshoot common issues that can arise in your concurrent Elixir application, turning frowns upside down (and getting your application running smoothly again).

Understanding Common Culprits:

1. **Race Conditions:** Imagine two chefs trying to grab the last egg at the same time. In a concurrent application, a race condition occurs when multiple processes try to access or modify the same data concurrently, potentially leading to unexpected results.

- **Example:** Process A reads the value of a counter, increments it by 1, and writes the new value back. But before process A can write the new value, process B also reads the counter, increments it by 1 (using the old value), and writes its own incremented value. This could result in the counter being incremented by only 1 instead of 2, as intended.

2. **Deadlocks:** Think of a deadlock as a Mexican standoff between processes. Two or more processes are waiting for each other to release resources they hold, creating a stalemate where no progress can be made.

- **Example:** Process A holds a lock on resource X and needs resource Y. Process B holds a lock on resource Y and needs resource X. Neither process can proceed, and the application grinds to a halt.

3. **Livelocks:** Imagine Sisyphus, forever pushing a boulder uphill, only to have it roll back down. Livelocks occur when processes are constantly busy but never making actual progress.

141

- **Example:** Two processes are constantly trying to acquire the same lock, but the lock becomes available only briefly between requests. This can lead to a loop where neither process can acquire the lock and complete its task.

Debugging Techniques:

1. **Logging and Tracing:** Logs and traces provide valuable insights into the execution flow of your application. By strategically placing log statements and utilizing tracing tools, you can identify where potential issues might be occurring and how processes are interacting.
- **Example:** Logging the state of a counter before and after each access can help identify race conditions. Tracing process interactions can reveal deadlocks or livelocks.
2. **Visualization Tools:** Sometimes, a picture is worth a thousand log messages. Tools like **dialyzer** or **creater** can visualize the message flow between processes in your application, making it easier to spot potential deadlocks or inefficiencies.
3. **Testing in Isolation:** While unit testing is crucial, consider creating tests that specifically target potential concurrency issues. Simulate race conditions or deadlocks in a controlled environment to identify and fix problems before they impact your production system.

Debugging concurrent applications requires patience and a methodical approach. By understanding common pitfalls and utilizing the right tools, you can effectively troubleshoot issues and ensure your concurrent application runs smoothly.

Additional Tips:

- Use well-defined synchronization mechanisms like mutexes and semaphores to control access to shared data and avoid race conditions.
- Carefully design your process interactions to minimize the risk of deadlocks.
- Implement timeouts or backoff strategies to prevent livelocks from occurring.

Additional Examples and Code for Debugging Concurrent Issues

1. Identifying Race Conditions with Logs:

Elixir

```elixir
defmodule Counter do

  use Agent

  def start_link(_) do

    Agent.start_link(fn -> 0 end)

  end

  def increment(pid) do

    Agent.get_and_update(pid, &(&1 + 1))

  end

end
```

```elixir
end

defmodule MyApp do

  def start_link(_) do

    counter_pid = Counter.start_link()

    spawn(fn -> loop(counter_pid) end)

    spawn(fn -> loop(counter_pid) end)

  end

  defp loop(counter_pid) do

    IO.puts "Current value: #{Counter.increment(counter_pid)}"

    Process.sleep(100)

  end

end
```

This example demonstrates a potential race condition. Two spawned processes call **Counter.increment** concurrently, which might not always result in an accurate incremented value due to the lack of proper synchronization.

Running this code and analyzing the logs (printed by **IO.puts**) might show inconsistencies in the counter's value, indicating a race condition.

2. Visualizing Deadlocks with dialyzer:

Elixir

```elixir
defmodule ResourceA do
  def acquire do
    # Simulate acquiring a resource (e.g., database lock)
    Process.sleep(1000)
  end
  def release do
    # Simulate releasing a resource
  end
end

defmodule ResourceB do
  def acquire do
    # Simulate acquiring a resource
    Process.sleep(1000)
  end
  def release do
    # Simulate releasing a resource
  end
```

```elixir
end

defmodule Worker do

  def start_link do

    spawn(fn -> loop() end)

  end

  defp loop do

    ResourceA.acquire()

    ResourceB.acquire()

    # Do some work

    ResourceB.release()

    ResourceA.release()

  end

end
```

This example creates a potential deadlock scenario. Both **ResourceA** and **ResourceB** acquisition involve a delay, and **Worker** tries to acquire them in a specific order.

Using **dialyzer** on this code might reveal a deadlock, as both processes wait for each other to release resources they hold.

3. Testing for Livelocks with ExUnit:

Elixir

```elixir
defmodule MyConcurrentFunctionTest do
  use ExUnit.Case

  test "avoids livelock when acquiring a lock" do
    with_capture do
      spawn(fn ->
        loop(fn -> MyModule.critical_section() end)
      end)
      spawn(fn ->
        loop(fn -> MyModule.critical_section() end)
      end)
      # Wait for some time to allow potential livelock to occur
      Process.sleep(1000)
    end
    refuted captured_output?("Failed to acquire lock")
  end

  defp loop(operation) do
    case operation.() do
      {:ok, _} -> loop(operation)
```

```
    {:error, _} -> :ok   # Handle lock acquisition failure
(e.g., with backoff)

  end

  end

end
```

This example utilizes **ExUnit** to test if a potential livelock occurs when acquiring a lock within a critical section of code (**MyModule.critical_section**). The test verifies if any process logs a "Failed to acquire lock" message repeatedly, indicating a livelock situation.

These are just a few examples to illustrate debugging techniques for concurrent issues. The specific approach will depend on the nature of the problem you're encountering. By combining logging, tracing, visualization tools, and well-structured tests, you can effectively debug and resolve concurrency challenges in your Elixir applications.

By following these strategies, you can transform debugging concurrent applications from a frustrating experience into a detective adventure where you uncover the root cause of issues and emerge victorious (with a well-functioning application).

Chapter 10: Conquering Concurrency with Elixir's Power Tools

You've mastered the fundamentals of building concurrent applications in Elixir – juggling tasks like a pro! But there's a whole world of advanced features and best practices waiting to be explored. Buckle up, because in this chapter, we're diving deep into Elixir's OTP library and uncovering techniques to make your concurrent applications run smoother than a freshly Zamboni-ed ice rink (metaphor alert!).

10.1 Advanced OTP Features: GenEvent, GenStage, and Beyond

Elixir's OTP library goes beyond just processes and supervisors. It offers a rich set of powerful tools designed to streamline communication, data processing, and overall application structure in your concurrent Elixir applications. Let's explore some of these gems and how they can elevate your development experience.

1. GenEvent: The Central Nervous System of Your Application

Imagine a well-coordinated event system for your application. GenEvent provides a structured way to publish and handle events. Processes can subscribe to specific events, allowing them to react and perform actions only when relevant information is published. This loose coupling between processes promotes modularity and maintainability.

- **Benefits:**
    - ○ Improved scalability – Processes only handle events they care about, reducing unnecessary workload.
    - ○ Easier debugging – Event flow becomes more explicit, simplifying issue identification.
    - ○ Enhanced testability – You can isolate event handling logic for individual processes.

Code Example (Publishing and Handling Events with GenEvent):

Elixir

```elixir
defmodule MyApp do

  use GenEvent

  def start_link(_) do

    GenEvent.cast({:source, "Hello, world!"})

    {:ok, pid}

  end

end
```

```elixir
defmodule MyEventHandler do

  use GenEvent

  def handle_event({:source, message}, _state) do

    IO.puts "Received message: #{message}"

  end

  def subscribe(server_pid) do

    GenEvent.add_handler(server_pid, self())

  end

end
```

In this example, **MyApp** publishes an event with the message "Hello, world!". **MyEventHandler** subscribes to this event and handles it by printing the message.

2. GenStage: Building Efficient Data Pipelines

Data processing is often a core function in concurrent applications. GenStage allows you to create modular processing stages that handle data transformations in a sequential manner. Stages are connected to form a pipeline, where the output of one stage becomes the input for the next.

- **Benefits:**

- Improved code organization – Data processing logic is broken down into smaller, reusable stages.
- Enhanced flexibility – Stages can be easily added, removed, or replaced without impacting the entire pipeline.
- Scalability – Stages can be distributed across multiple processes for improved performance.

Code Example (Simple Data Processing Pipeline with GenStage):

Elixir

```elixir
defmodule DataProcessor do

  use GenStage

  def init(_) do

    {:ok, []}

  end

  def handle_call({:transform, data}, _from, state) do

    {:noreply, [{:data, transformed_data(data)} | state]}

  end
```

152

```
# Define the transform_data function to perform specific
processing

defp transformed_data(data) do

  data * 2

end

end
```

This example shows a basic **GenStage** that doubles the value of incoming data. You can chain multiple stages together to create complex data processing pipelines.

3. Beyond the Basics: More OTP Goodies

The OTP library offers a treasure trove of tools beyond GenEvent and GenStage. Here's a quick glimpse at some others you might encounter:

- **GenServer:** Provides a structured way to manage state and handle function calls for concurrent access.
- **Task:** Facilitates creating lightweight background jobs for short-lived tasks, perfect for offloading non-critical work.
- **Supervisor:** Helps define hierarchical process supervision trees, ensuring application robustness by restarting child processes that fail unexpectedly.t.

By leveraging these advanced OTP features, you can build scalable, maintainable, and efficient concurrent applications that effectively handle complex tasks and data flows. Stay tuned as we explore even more ways to master concurrency in Elixir!

10.2 Performance Optimization Techniques for Concurrent Applications

Building performant concurrent applications in Elixir requires careful consideration. Just like a Formula One race car needs fine-tuning for peak performance, your concurrent applications can benefit from optimization techniques to run smoothly and efficiently. Here, we'll explore some key strategies to keep your applications in the winner's circle.

1. Leverage Lightweight Processes:

One of Elixir's strengths is its use of lightweight processes. Unlike traditional threads, which can be resource-intensive, Elixir processes have a smaller footprint. This allows you to create many smaller, focused processes instead of a few heavyweight ones. Imagine having a team of synchronized swimmers – each performing their part efficiently, contributing to the overall performance.

- **Benefit**: By utilizing smaller processes, you can distribute workload effectively, leading to faster overall execution.

2. Optimize Message Passing:

Communication between processes is essential in concurrent applications. However, sending large chunks of data back and forth can create bottlenecks. Here are some tips for efficient message passing:

- **Use Efficient Data Structures:** Choose data structures that are well-suited for the type of data you're sending. For example, use maps or lists instead of complex nested structures that require more processing to unpack.
- **Consider Lazy Evaluation:** If a message payload only needs to be partially processed initially, consider using lazy evaluation techniques. This can defer processing of unnecessary data until it's actually required.

Code Example (Using a Map for Efficient Data):

Elixir

```elixir
def send_user_data(user_id, %{name: name, email: email}) do

  # Efficient message with relevant data

end
```

In this example, a map is used to send user data, containing only the necessary fields (**name** and **email**).

3. Utilize Supervision Trees:

Elixir's OTP library provides powerful supervision capabilities. By designing well-structured supervision trees, you can ensure the overall health and robustness of your application. A supervision tree defines how child processes are monitored and restarted in case of failures.

- **Benefit:** Proper supervision helps isolate failures and prevent them from cascading, keeping your application running even if individual processes encounter issues.

Code Example (Simple Supervision Tree):

Elixir

```elixir
defmodule MyApp do

  use Supervisor

  def init(_) do

    worker = WorkerSupervisor.start_link()

    children = [worker: worker]

    {:ok, children, strategy: :one_for_one}

  end

end
```

This example shows a simple supervisor tree with a single child process (**worker**). If the **worker** process crashes, the supervisor can restart it automatically.

4. Embrace Functional Programming Principles:

Functional programming concepts like immutability and avoiding side effects can contribute to performance optimization in concurrent applications.

- **Immutability:** When working with data, consider using immutable data structures whenever possible. This helps prevent race conditions and makes reasoning about concurrent access easier. Imagine a library with a single copy of a book – everyone can read it, but no one can accidentally modify it (unless there's a rogue pen floating around!).
- **Avoiding Side Effects:** Functions with side effects (like modifying global state) can be harder to reason about in a concurrent context. By relying on pure functions that produce predictable outputs for a given input, you can improve code clarity and potentially avoid performance issues.

Performance optimization is an ongoing process. By employing these techniques, measuring results, and continuously refining your approach, you can ensure your concurrent Elixir applications deliver exceptional performance.

10.3 Best Practices for Using Concurrency Effectively in Elixir Projects

Building robust and maintainable concurrent applications in Elixir requires following some key principles. These best practices will serve as a compass, guiding you towards creating well-structured and performant applications that can handle the complexities of concurrency.

1. Focus on Modularity:

- **Concept:** Break down your application logic into smaller, independent processes that communicate through well-defined message passing. This modular approach promotes code reusability, easier testing, and improved maintainability. Imagine building a house with pre-fabricated walls – each wall is a well-defined unit that can be assembled efficiently into the final structure.

Code Example (Modular Processes with Message Passing):

Elixir

```elixir
defmodule OrderProcessor do

 def start_link(_) do

  spawn(fn -> listen_for_orders() end)

 end

 defp listen_for_orders do

  receive do

            {:new_order, order_data} ->
process_order(order_data)

  end

  listen_for_orders()
```

```
end

defp process_order(order_data) do

  # Perform order processing logic

  GenEvent.cast({:order_processed, order_data})

end

end

defmodule InventoryManager do

  def handle_event({:order_processed, order_data}) do

    update_inventory(order_data)

  end

end
```

In this example, **OrderProcessor** listens for new order messages and processes them. It then publishes an event (**:order_processed**) that the **InventoryManager** can handle to update inventory levels.

2. Embrace Immutability:

- **Concept:** Whenever possible, utilize immutable data structures like lists, maps, and structs. This helps prevent race conditions and makes your code easier to reason about. With immutable data, you create a new copy of the data with any modifications, rather than changing the original data itself. Imagine a recipe – you can make multiple copies with slight variations (adding spices!), but the original recipe remains unchanged.

Code Example (Using Maps for Immutable Data):

Elixir

```elixir
def update_user_info(user_id, updates) do

  user = get_user(user_id)

  updated_user = Map.merge(user, updates)

  update_user_in_db(updated_user)

end
```

This example retrieves a user record, merges it with the updates in a new map (**updated_user**), and then updates the database with the new data. The original user data remains unchanged.

3. Test Thoroughly:

- **Concept:** Thorough testing is crucial for concurrent applications. Utilize unit tests, integration tests, and property-based testing to ensure your application behaves as expected under various scenarios, especially when multiple processes are involved. Imagine a well-oiled machine – each part needs to be tested individually and together to ensure smooth operation.

Code Example (Unit Testing a Process Function):

Elixir

```elixir
defmodule OrderProcessorTest do

  use ExUnit.Case

  test "processes new orders" do

    {:ok, pid} = OrderProcessor.start_link()

    send(pid, {:new_order, %{name: "T-Shirt", quantity: 1}})

    # Assert expected behavior after sending the message

  end

end
```

This example demonstrates a unit test for the **OrderProcessor** process, verifying its behavior when receiving a new order message.

4. Leverage OTP Supervision:

- **Concept:** Effectively utilize OTP's supervision capabilities to manage process life cycles. Design well-structured supervision trees to ensure graceful handling of process failures. This helps prevent cascading failures and keeps your application running smoothly even if individual processes encounter issues. Imagine a team with a backup plan − if someone gets sick, others can step in to ensure the work continues.

5. Monitor and Log Strategically:

- **Concept:** Implement strategic monitoring and logging practices to gain insights into your application's behavior. Monitor process health, message flow, and resource utilization. Utilize logs to record important events and aid in debugging potential issues. Imagine having a control panel for your application – you can monitor various aspects and identify areas that need attention.

By following these best practices, you'll be well on your way to building exceptional concurrent applications in Elixir. Remember, concurrency is a powerful tool, and these practices will help you harness its potential effectively!

10.4 Identifying and Avoiding Anti-Patterns in Elixir Concurrency

The exciting world of concurrency also comes with potential pitfalls. Just like a well-maintained garden needs weed removal, your concurrent Elixir applications benefit from identifying and avoiding anti-patterns. These are common design flaws that can lead to performance issues, maintainability problems, and unexpected behavior. Let's explore some key anti-patterns to keep an eye out for:

1. The Chatty Processes:

- **Anti-Pattern:** Processes constantly sending unnecessary messages to each other can overwhelm the message queue and lead to performance degradation. Imagine a group chat where everyone messages every second, even for trivial updates. It becomes overwhelming and hard to follow the conversation.

- **Solution:** Design your communication patterns to be efficient. Processes should only send messages when necessary and relevant information needs to be shared. Utilize techniques like pattern matching and filtering to avoid sending unnecessary messages.

Code Example (Avoiding Unnecessary Messages):

Elixir

```elixir
defmodule OrderProcessor do

  def handle_event({:new_order, order_data} = msg when order_data.status == :paid) do

    process_order(order_data)

  end

  def handle_event(_msg), do: :ok  # Ignore irrelevant messages

end
```

In this example, **OrderProcessor** only handles new order events where the order status is paid. This avoids processing unnecessary messages for unpaid orders.

2. The Global State Monster:

- **Anti-Pattern:** Creating a giant ball of global state that all processes need to access can lead to race conditions and difficulty managing the application's state. Imagine a single whiteboard for everyone's notes – it becomes messy, confusing, and prone to accidental overwrites.
- **Solution:** Break down your application state into smaller, manageable parts. Utilize local process state, ETS tables for frequently accessed data, or GenServer for managing state with controlled access.

3. The Overcomplicated Supervisor Tree:

- **Anti-Pattern:** While supervision trees are powerful, excessively complex structures can be difficult to manage and understand. Imagine a nested hierarchy of supervisors so intricate that it becomes unclear who supervises whom.
- **Solution:** Design clear and focused supervision trees. Group related processes under appropriate supervisors and avoid unnecessary nesting. Keep it simple and maintainable.

Code Example (Simple vs. Overcomplicated Supervision Tree):

Elixir

Simple Tree

defmodule MyApp do

  use Supervisor

```elixir
  def init(_) do

    worker1 = Worker1.start_link()

    worker2 = Worker2.start_link()

    children = [worker1: worker1, worker2: worker2]

    {:ok, children, strategy: :one_for_one}

  end

end

# Overcomplicated Tree (avoid this!)

defmodule MyApp do

  use Supervisor

  def init(_) do

      # Deeply nested hierarchy with multiple supervisor levels

  end

end
```

4. The Long-Running Process:

- **Anti-Pattern:** Processes that perform long-running tasks can block other processes waiting for them to finish. This can lead to reduced responsiveness and potential deadlocks. Imagine a process stuck in an infinite loop, holding up the entire system.
- **Solution:** Break down long-running tasks into smaller chunks. Utilize GenStage or Tasks to handle long-running operations asynchronously, freeing up the process for other work.

5. The Copy-Paste Syndrome:

- **Anti-Pattern:** Copying and pasting boilerplate code for concurrency patterns across your application can lead to code duplication and difficulty in maintenance.
- **Solution:** Leverage OTP features and libraries like GenEvent, GenStage, and GenServer to handle common concurrency patterns. This promotes code reuse and simplifies maintenance.

By being aware of these anti-patterns and adopting best practices, you can develop robust and maintainable concurrent applications in Elixir. Remember, concurrency empowers you to create scalable and efficient systems, but careful planning and design are crucial for success.

Conclusion

You've embarked on a journey through the exciting world of concurrency in Elixir, and now you're equipped with the knowledge and skills to build powerful, scalable applications. Remember, concurrency is a superpower for handling complex tasks efficiently.

As you move forward, keep these key takeaways in mind:

- **Embrace Modularity:** Break down problems into smaller, well-defined processes that communicate effectively.
- **Leverage OTP Features:** Utilize the rich set of OTP tools like GenStage, GenServer, and GenEvent to streamline your development process.
- **Prioritize Performance:** Continuously strive to optimize your applications for efficiency and responsiveness.
- **Maintainability is Key:** Write clean, modular code that is easy to understand and maintain.
- **Embrace Functional Concepts:** Functional programming principles like immutability and higher-order functions can be powerful allies in your concurrent development journey.

The world of Elixir concurrency is vast and ever-evolving. Keep exploring, experiment with different techniques, and most importantly, have fun! There's no better way to solidify your understanding than by building real-world applications that leverage the power of concurrency.

So, go forth and conquer! The Elixir community awaits your contributions as you create innovative and scalable applications. Remember, the only limit is your imagination.